CLEVELAND'S CULTURAL GARDENS

CLEVELAND'S CULTURAL GARDENS

A Landscape of Diversity

JOHN J. GRABOWSKI AND LAUREN R. PACINI

THE KENT STATE UNIVERSITY PRESS · KENT, OHIO

Unless otherwise noted, all photographs are by Lauren R. Pacini.

ISBN 978-1-60635-441-4
Manufactured in the United States of America

Cataloging information for this title is available at the Library of Congress.

26 25 24 23 22 5 4 3 2 1

CONTENTS

ACKNOWLEDGMENTS

This book's origins date to the early 1970s when, as the ethnic archives specialist for the Western Reserve Historical Society, I accompanied a photographer to the Cultural Gardens to take images for use in an exhibit at the society. It was my first encounter with the site, belated and somewhat ironic given that I was a lifelong Clevelander. That visit would eventually lead to the WRHS's acquisition of the Cleveland Cultural Gardens Federation archives. And those archives were central to the creation of scholarly works written by John Bodnar, Mitch Berbrier, Mark Tebeau, and Sean Martin, which have served as central sources for the writing of this volume.

Yet, the immediate impetus for this book came from Lauren Pacini. Lauren and I had worked together on four previous volumes that focused on aspects of the history of Cleveland. It was Lauren who suggested that we create a new work on the Cultural Gardens, a landscape and a topic on which he had already set his lens. As author, I sincerely thank him for his partnership and his professionalism. So, this work is a partnership: a melding of Lauren's photography and his enthusiasm for the topic and my interest in examining the history of the gardens with a focus on their impact on a changing natural landscape, and on the national, international, and local events that shaped their creation and evolution, as well as on the manner in which people have chosen to see them.

Both of us have been supported by a number of individuals. Wael Khoury, president of the Cultural Gardens Federation, and Lori Ashyk, executive director of the Cultural Gardens Federation, were central supporters of Lauren's photographic work, and Lori encouraged both of us to pursue the creation of a book. Mitch Berbrier generously shared the unpublished manuscript of his history of the gardens, which provided important insights into the issues of race and ethnicity that have shaped and reshaped both their meaning and structure over time. Sean Martin's insights into the history of the Hebrew Garden were equally important. The historic images in this book derive almost entirely from the incredibly rich collections of the Western Reserve Historical Society. Ann Sindelar, reference supervisor for the society's library, deserves immense credit for getting the digital copies prepared and sent to the publisher during COVID-restricted operating hours and at a time when she had assumed multiple ancillary responsibilities.

Our most heartfelt acknowledgement, however, is to those who created the Cultural Gardens—migrants and immigrants and their offspring. In reshaping a city and a landscape, they have built a stunning monument to diversity—a symbol both of cultural memory and of hope.

John J. Grabowski

INTRODUCTION

The Cultural Gardens are collectively one of the landmarks of Cleveland, Ohio, and, indeed, each is arguably a unique global monument celebrating the diversity of the greater community—a celebration evoked in a combination of landscapes, sculptures, and plantings indigenous to particular countries and ethnicities. Currently, there are 33 individual gardens bordering Doan Brook along Martin Luther King Jr. Boulevard and East Boulevard. Begun in 1916 and "reborn," so to speak, near the turn of the current century, the gardens seem to suggest a sense of overall union among diverse cultures—each having arrived in Cleveland from a different place on the globe, ranging from Albania to Vietnam to Ethiopia. They posit harmony and structure, particularly in the sculptures they contain and their landscape design, and they evoke an assumed permanence of memory. Much of this volume, particularly the contemporary photographs, hint at this strong sense of connection via memory, via structure, and by landscape.

Yet the Cultural Gardens are but one appearance in time in a landscape centered on the Doan Brook valley, which dates back for millennia and which has been changed by nature and most recently by humans. We have modified it many times in terms of the lay of the land, its ecology, and the nature and purpose of the memorials and monuments that came to be placed on that landscape. How it has been utilized by humans is a product of many factors: some local, some national, and many global. Its utility has reflected the imperatives of many eras, from the time of Native American settlement to the needs of European fur trappers and then farmers. Its history, as a landscape of leisure and then of memory, has been equally varied—from a private park to a symbol of the City Beautiful movement to a memorial for those who died in World War I.

The Cultural Gardens represent the most recent reconstruction of the valley and, undoubtedly, are the most complex addition, being reflective of the global forces that have shifted patterns of migration and the politics that have shaped and continue to shape attitudes toward who should come and who can "belong" in a nation constructed by migration and immigration. Created during a global war, the gardens have again and again been portrayed and seen as a platform celebrating cultural diversity and—to use the Cold War phrase—"peaceful coexistence." However, they have been shaped and continuously reshaped by conflict. Indeed, they have seldom seen a period in which some of the cultures they represent were not engaged in ideological or actual battle. Two world wars and the long Cold War parallel a good part of their history, and those struggles are sometimes obliquely referenced by the monuments to national poets and national heroes in individual gardens.

In their local context, they also reflect on that perennial question of belonging, albeit acted out within the immediate community. After dedicating an initial monument to English culture, expressed in the 1916 Shakespeare Garden, they evolved into a commemoration of those groups (substantially European) that came, many via Ellis Island, in the years before the early 1920s. In fact, this version of inclusiveness was, in part, a worthy and healthy reaction to the restrictions placed on the immigration of many of those groups in 1917, 1921, and 1924. Essentially, it was this initial pushback, by a progressive city against a growing national narrative, that gave full meaning to the gardens. Yet, when the demographics of the city shifted with the Great Migration of African Americans, it took time for the Cultural Gardens to accommodate this change, and it is only recently that they have come to reflect the global shift in emigration from countries outside of Europe following the change of the national immigration law in 1965.

The landscape of the valley, defined largely by the memorials placed within it, will continue to change, driven not only by shifts in immigration but also by the attitudes expressed about those who transit from nation to nation. This book is not simply the story of the Cultural Gardens, but it is also the history of the wider landscape in which they are situated, what nature has made of it, and how we have decided to change it—at multiple times and for multiple purposes. Only Doan Brook, which still defines the long linear area in which the gardens have been set, seems to have a permanence of sorts. That ongoing modification has been the product of contention and cooperation, of politics and policies, and of the imperatives created by continually changing urban infrastructures. It is a story that reflects a larger history—of the city, of the nation, and of the world—and it is that wider story, along with that of the brook, that are central to this book.

There are many ways to view the history of the Cleveland Cultural Gardens, and this work is certainly not the first, nor will it be the last.[1] Other works have informed it, and new essays continue to be written. Those that are available were critical to the creation of the text for this volume.

The history of the Cultural Gardens was first detailed by Clara Lederer's *Their Paths Are Peace.* Published in 1954, it considers the history of the gardens up to that time, and in its own way it was impelled by its times, the era of the Cold War that followed World War II. Critical academic attention to the gardens began in 1992 with John Bodnar's focus on the gardens in chapter 4 of his book *Remaking America: Public Memory, Commemoration, and Patriotism in the Twentieth Century.* Bodnar's chapter argues for the unique role of the gardens, which assumed their current form in the 1920s, a very troubled time in American history. In 2010, Sean Martin addressed the intersection of the Jewish community with Rockefeller Park and the gardens in *Cleveland's Land of Promise: Rockefeller Park and the Jewish Community.* His is a story of public space within a community that was then primarily Jewish. Also in 2010, Mark Tebeau's "Sculpted Landscapes: Art & Place in Cleveland's Cultural Gardens, 1916–2006" appeared in the *Journal of Social History.* Tebeau's article is an excellent detailed look, not only at the history of the system of gardens but also of the times in which they were created and more particularly their relationships to wider trends in design and structure as well as their place in the history of memory and memorialization. These works were joined several years later (2012 and 2013) by two published essays, by Professor Mitch Berbrier, which explore the relationship of the Cultural Gardens to peace and intercommunal understanding. Berbrier also assisted in the research for this book by sharing an unpublished manuscript history of the gardens that he had prepared.

Each of these works has served to inform the narrative presented in this volume—as do the black-and-white contemporary photographs by Lauren R. Pacini. It was his idea that a new, highly illustrated history of the Cultural Gardens be prepared. His images are the core of this narrative as they serve to define the structure and look of the gardens as they are today. They also help explicate the trends in design that, at particular times, were selected as the best way to honor a culture. In that sense, the images parallel a text that focuses on the continuous change of a landscape and a landmark—a unique place within the American landscape.

CHAPTER 1

THE DOAN BROOK VALLEY BEFORE EUROPEAN SETTLEMENT

In a strange way, Doan Brook today is a reminder of Cleveland's prehistoric past because, outside of the Cuyahoga and Rocky Rivers, it is still a relatively open, albeit secondary, waterway in or near the city.[1] Other waterways, including Walworth Run, Burke Brook, Giddings Brook, Dugway Brook, and Nine Mile Creek, are now largely confined within culverts or have been redirected. How and why Doan Brook managed to survive is an intimate part of the larger history of what is now the site of the Cultural Gardens. To begin to fully understand the history of the brook and its valley, we need to consider the first people who saw and used it.

All the waterways in the Cleveland area were the product of the end of the great Ice Age some 15,000 years ago. As the ice retreated to the north from its southern edge near present-day Akron, Ohio, those features that created the area's landscape slowly emerged. Millennia later, after European settlement in the area, the landscape began to be manipulated, slowly at first and then, in some instances, into oblivion. Doan Brook has survived, although it, too, has been routed through tunnels in spots and confined by stone walls in other places, most notably within the Cultural Gardens.

Water and a warming climate brought the first people to the area that is now home to the Cultural Gardens to hunt and forage for food. The earliest human habitation in northeast Ohio took

These items found at the site of the Rockefeller Park Greenhouse are evidence of Native American settlement in the Doan Brook valley. The pottery, beads, and arrow point date to circa 1500 AD; the notched drill base most likely dates to about 3000 BC. Other items from the site—including a handful of small animal and fish bones, flint flakes, and fragments of freshwater mussels—indicate that it was the location of a small village in the 1500s. (Courtesy of the Cleveland Museum of Natural History)

place nearly 10,000 years ago. At that point, it was largely nomadic, but evidence shows that the earliest settlers had come from the southern areas beyond what had been the edge of the glaciers that covered the region. Native American settlement would slowly shift from hunter-gatherers to more settled groups and eventually in what is known as the Whittlesey Tradition period (1000 to 1640 AD) to longer term settlements, which began to be established around 1500 AD and relied on farming. During this period of Native American presence in the area, habitation and settlement would ebb and flow. What was a constant for all the first people, however, was water: for drinking; perhaps more importantly, as a resource that expedited movement; and as a site for settlement.[2]

It is impossible to know for certain who were the first people to have encountered what would come to be known as Doan Brook, nor do we have any idea as to what name they may have given the waterway. Artifacts have been found along the brook, so we know it was part of this earlier period of human settlement. Then, as now, the waterway originated in the bluestone heights above Cleveland,

Doan Brook as it is seen today, constrained by walls as it wends its way through Rockefeller Park.

The Doan Valley Tunnel under construction beneath University Circle below the Portage Escarpment.

part of the Portage Escarpment that was the western section of the Appalachian Plateau. It flowed from several sources in what is now Shaker Heights and moved along a relatively easy route through the heavy forests that had come to cover the area in the centuries after the Ice Age. It descended then, as it does now, from the escarpment to the lowlands below into what is now known as University Circle. Those lowlands had been the bottom of the lakes that once covered the area and had receded over the centuries. The soil in the old lake beds is sandy—a feature apparent in any major construction excavation in the area today. In the centuries that followed, nutrient-rich topsoil was created above it and would turn out to be fertile farmland for the first European settlers.

Waterways that entered Lake Erie, such as Doan Brook, Nine Mile Creek, Euclid Creek, the Cuyahoga River, and the Rocky River, often also hosted Native American settlements at their intersection with the lakeshore—again, a function of travel but also a place to catch fish. While the waterways formed an access route for north-south travel, the old ridge lines left by the retreating lake waters provided an east-west route and often served as sites for temporary settlements. Those ridgelines would eventually become roads, including Euclid Avenue, Detroit Avenue, and the aptly named Center Ridge Road. One Native American route, later named the Mahoning Trail, stretched from what is now downtown Cleveland southward along what is now Broadway Avenue to the Portage trail near Akron, and it became a major transport route for the exchange of goods. A branch trail from Doan Brook in University Circle intersected with that trail in what became Newburg Township, today part of the Slavic Village area. The first northerly segment followed what is approximately East 105th Street, essentially the first segment of the Opportunity Corridor.[3]

The physical portage where canoes would be carried and portage, which formed the southern end of the trail, was the divide between two hydrographic systems. Rivers to the north flowed to Lake Erie. Those to the south eventually came to the Ohio River. By taking a canoe up to the divide, one carried it over and then proceeded south by another river system. It was a path that was eventually mimicked by the Ohio & Erie Canal, in route and in purpose: both served to foster commerce and communication.

The Opportunity Corridor, a limited-access roadway and with multipurpose paths, will connect I-77/I-490 and University Circle.

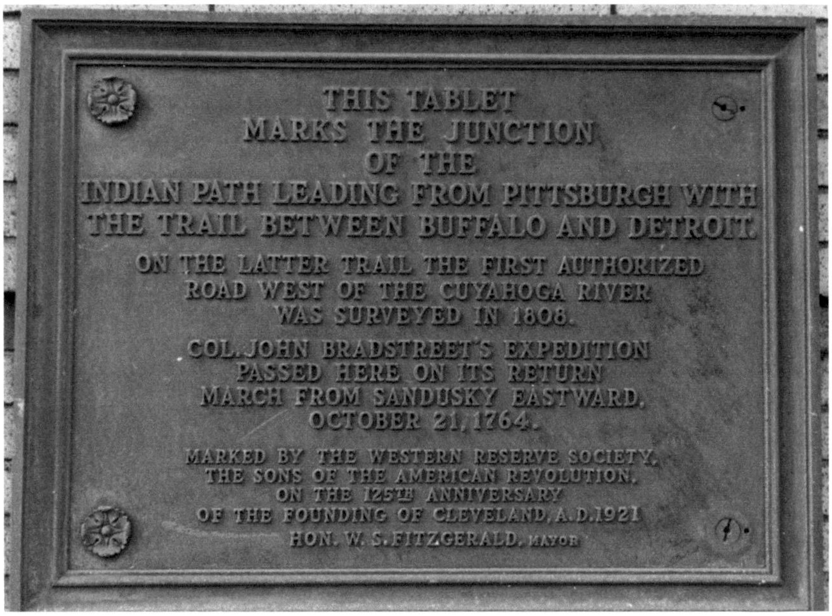

This plaque, which once was located at West Twenty-Fifth Street and Detroit Avenue, is a reminder of the way Native American trails evolved into some of the major roads in Cleveland. (Courtesy of the Western Reserve Historical Society)

Native American habitations, ranging from early campsites to walled villages, dotted northeast Ohio and have revealed an evolving pattern of sophistication over time as well as changing settlement patterns. Burial mounds and encampments were discovered by the earliest settlers in Cleveland. Some were carefully (at least by the standards of the period) opened, with the objects discovered eventually finding their way to museum collections. Others were plowed under. Charles Whittlesey, the founder of the Western Reserve Historical Society and a noted geologist, prepared detailed maps of many sites and drawings of the objects found there. Today, these essays and drawings from the middle of the nineteenth century provide a guide to the complexity of human life in the region long before it was settled by Europeans.[4]

The first European encounters with the region may likely have taken place by the mid-seventeenth century when French Jesuit missionaries traveled along Lake Erie and wrote descriptions of the south shore of the lake. By the 1740s, French fur traders had established a post around 5 to 8 miles up the Cuyahoga River. Around 1750, an English trader, George Croghan, took up residence at the mouth of the Cuyahoga. By this period, northeast Ohio had become part of the colonial contention between the English and the French, and contacts with native Americans increased. Trading, particularly in furs, and travel through the area would further increase after the English victory of 1763 in the French and Indian War.

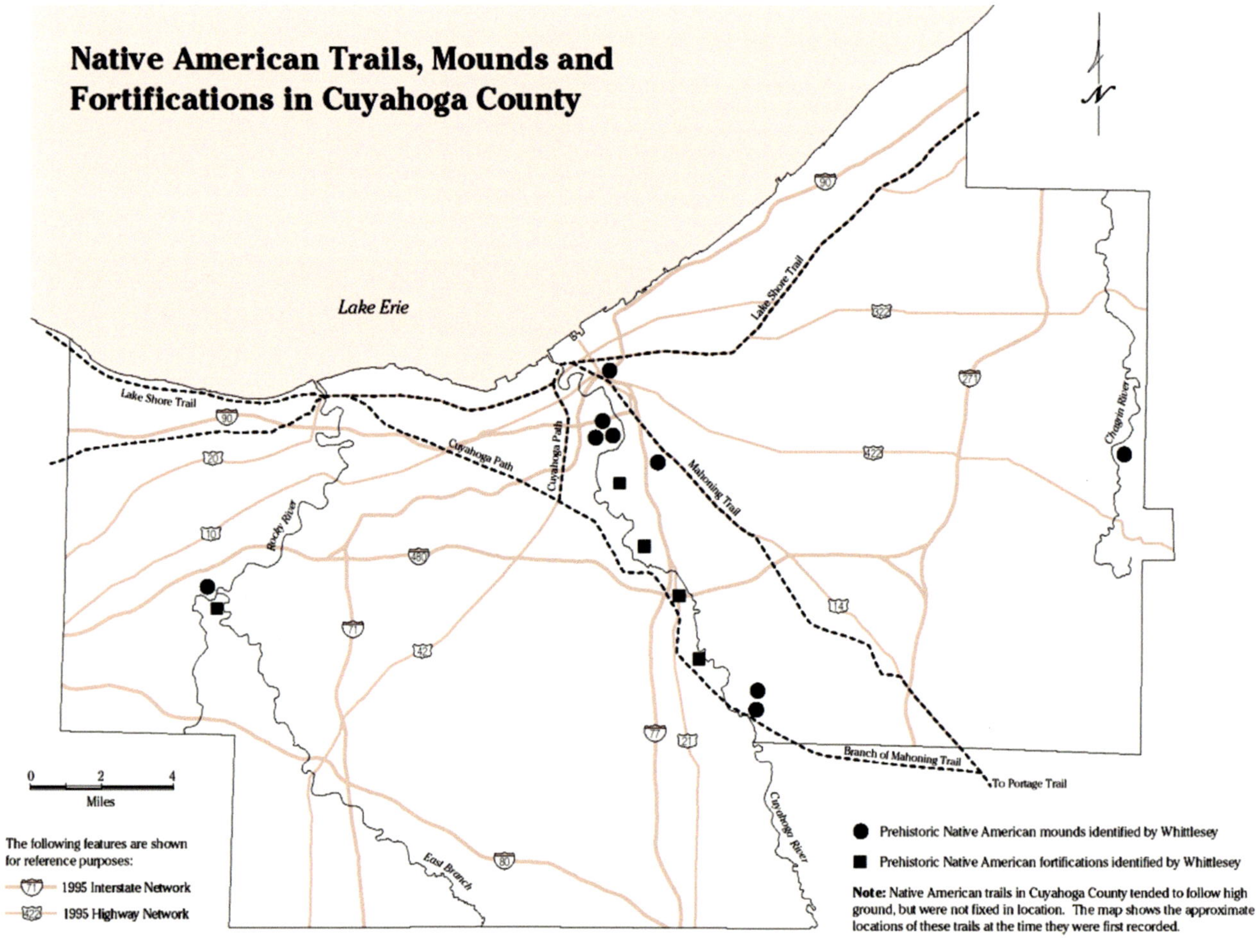

(Courtesy of *Encyclopedia of Cleveland History*)

While we have no direct evidence of early European visits to the Doan Brook area, we do know what the flora and fauna of the region were like. When the Western Reserve was surveyed in 1796 and 1797, the surveyors made notes regarding the natural resources they encountered. From their notes, we know that approximately 94 percent of the entire area of the reserve was covered by forests comprised of 26 varieties of trees, with beech being the most common. There were numerous Native American paths in addition to the main arteries previously noted, but no areas that had been fully cleared by the natives were listed. Essentially, the ecosystem seen at that time had not yet been tampered with by humans. Our best guess at what the lower Doan Brook valley looked like was that of a forested wetland with trees and an undergrowth of berries. Wildlife was abundant and included deer, bears, wild turkeys, squirrels, snakes, and a variety of rodents. The brook would have teamed with fish. The valley would have looked as it

Historic Lock 34 and Lockkeeper's House at 7104 Canal Road on the Ohio & Erie Canal.

had for many hundreds of years. The lake bed soil in what is now University Circle hosted large groves of black oak trees. Almost everywhere in the reserve the first surveyors found an unbelievable abundance: a white oak "14 ½ feet around the stump and I believe 50 feet without a limb and as straight as an arrow," another white oak "22 ½ feet around the trunk," and small trees "as thick set as the hair on a dog's back."[5] It was an abundance that would rather quickly disappear once settlement began in earnest in the 1800s.

Ironically, by the time these European observations of the landscape were made, the Native American presence in the Greater Cleveland area had dwindled, a process that began in the mid-1700s. Impelled by conflicts between the Iroquois nation in the east and the Senecas to the west as well as the French and Indian War in which the French and British made alliances with various native nations, the area had become a sort of demilitarized zone.

At the end of the American Revolution, the United States acquired sovereignty over the lands west of the Appalachians, stretching to the Mississippi River under the Treaty of Paris in 1784. Much of this land, including northeast Ohio, was still subject to Native American claim. However, in 1795, much of northeast Ohio's status as native-owned land would be extinguished by the Greenville Treaty that followed the defeat of a western Native American coalition by the United States at the Battle of Fallen Timbers (near Toledo) in 1794. This opened a segment of the Connecticut Western Reserve. The entire reserve, approximately 3 million acres, was part of Connecticut's old colonial claims that it had been able to retain after the creation of the United States. Now that Native American claim to at least two-thirds of it has been extinguished, the state sold the land to the Connecticut Land Company, a consortium of 56 men. For the state, the sale provided funds for operating its schools. For the partners of the company, it represented a speculative purchase that could potentially provide a huge profit as land-hungry Americans looked westward for more and better land to farm. The company appointed one of its members, Moses Cleaveland (a lawyer and Revolutionary War veteran), to head a party tasked with surveying the land.[6]

A year later, when Moses Cleaveland led his survey party to the Western Reserve, he conferenced with representatives of the Six Nations (Iroquois) near Buffalo. The Iroquois were not a party to the Greenville Treaty, and Cleaveland needed to negotiate with the tribe. He made an agreement with them that negated any claim they had to what was the eastern part of the Connecticut Western Reserve, giving 500 pounds of New York money, two beef cattle, trinkets, and 100 gallons of whiskey in return for any rights they had to the area. A member of Cleveland's survey party, John Holley, took notes at the meeting of a speech made by Red Jacket, an orator of the Six Nations and a sachem of the Senecas. Red Jacket noted:

> You white people make a great parade about religion, you say you have a book of laws and rules which was given you by the Great Spirit, but is this true? No says he, it was written by your own people. They do it to deceive you. Their whole wishes center here (pointing to his pocket), all they want is the money. . . . He says white people tell them, they wish to come and live among them as brothers, and learn them agriculture. So they bring on implements of husbandry and presents, tell them good stories and all appears honest. But when they are gone all appears as a dream. Our land is taken from us, and still we don't know how to farm it.[7]

Red Jacket, or Sagoyewatha (1750–1830), was a noted Seneca orator and major figure in relations between Native Americans and Europeans in the late eighteen and early nineteenth century. This image derives from an 1835 lithograph by Henry Corbould, which was based on a painting by Charles Bird King. (Courtesy of Wikipedia)

Later in the journey, as Cleaveland's party entered what would become Ohio at Conneaut Creek, another meeting was held with the Massagoes, who challenged his party's right to the land and negotiated a solution assuring "them that they should not be disturbed in their possessions, [for] we would treat them and their friends as our brothers." Paqua, one of the Native Americans, presented the surveyor with a "curious" pipe of peace and friendship, and Cleaveland gave the natives "a chain of wampum, silver trinkets, and other presents, and whiskey, to the amount of about twenty-five dollars."[8] Today, that peace pipe is at the Western Reserve Historical Society and is featured in its *Cleveland Starts Here* exhibit.

The arrival of the survey party in the Western Reserve in 1796 marked the beginning of a period in the history of enormous change in the natural landscape. What had existed for millennia would, during slightly over two centuries, be transformed. It would be a period in which Doan Brook would receive its name and eventually become the site of parks and monuments, among them the Cultural Gardens. In 2020, the Cultural Gardens Federation approved the establishment of a new Native American Garden.

CHAPTER 2

THE GOOD EARTH

In mid-July 1796, Moses Cleaveland and members of his survey party sailed along the south shore of Lake Erie seeking the mouth of the Cuyahoga River. Guided by old maps, they felt that it would be a good site to begin their survey. It was situated at the western boundary of that portion of the Connecticut Western Reserve free of Native American claim, and the river appeared to offer easy transit into the hinterlands.

As they approached the Cuyahoga, they would have passed the mouths of other rivers and streams. From east to west, those waterways were what would come to be known as the Grand River, Chagrin River, Euclid Creek, Nine Mile Creek, Dugway Brook, Doan Brook, and Giddings Brook. Cleaveland's party likely looked at each of these to ascertain whether they were the Cuyahoga.

When they came to the Cuyahoga River on July 22, they found its mouth heavily silted, but they moved beyond the sandbar up the river, docked, climbed up the hilly east bank (near where West St. Clair Avenue is now located), and set up camp on the higher land. Eventually, Cleaveland would decide that this site along the river was the best possible place to begin his survey of the land, given that the Cuyahoga River did, indeed, provide access to the interior of the Reserve. At the suggestions of his surveyors, the unofficial capital of the Connecticut Western Reserve was named after him.

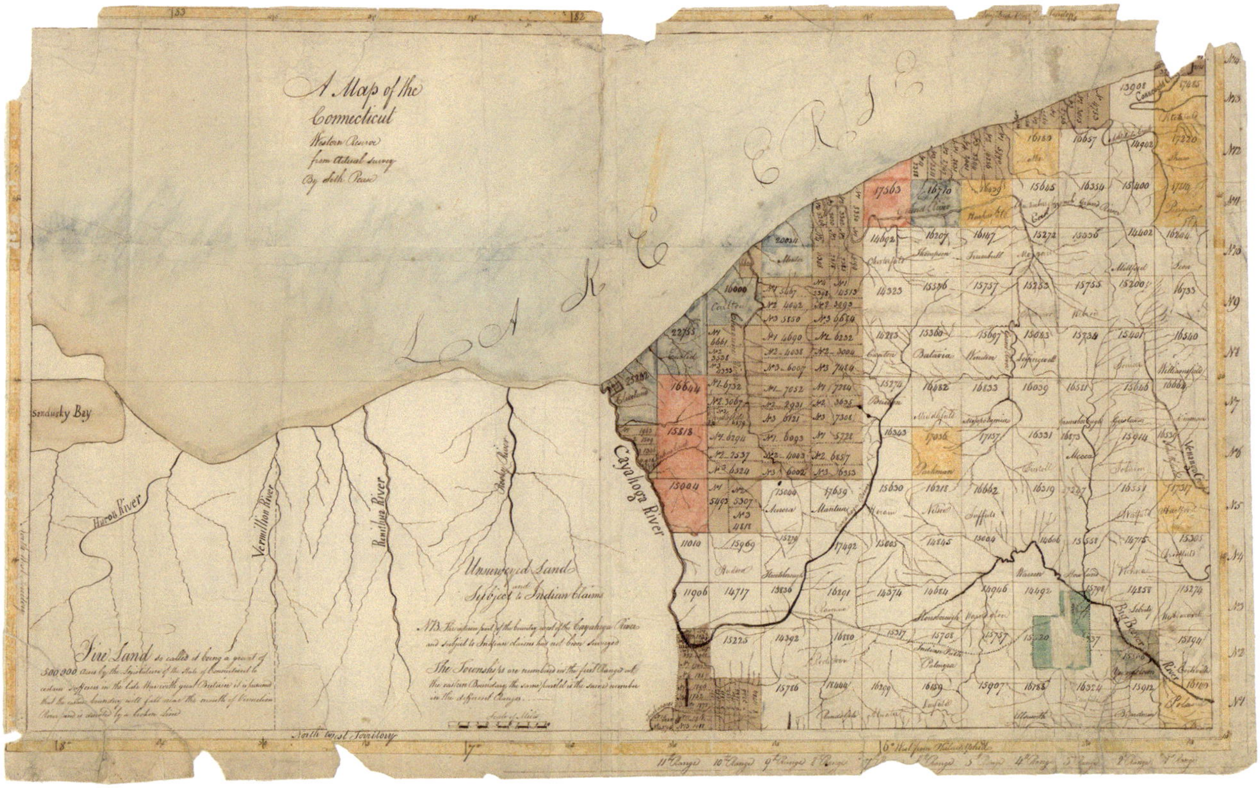

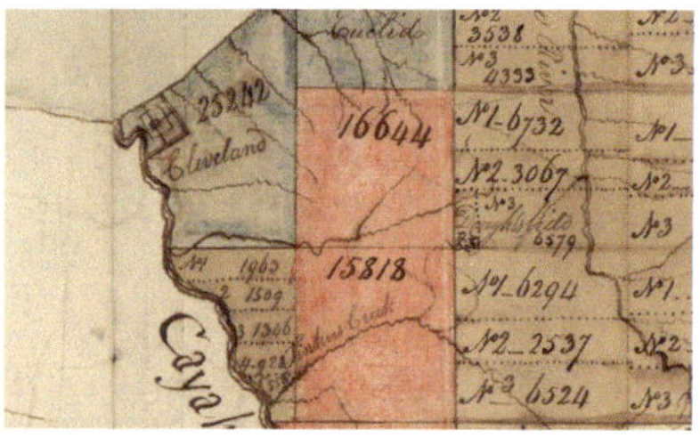

Top: Seth Pease 1797 map of the Western Reserve. (Courtesy of the Western Reserve Historical Society)

Above: Detail of Seth Pease's 1797 map showing waterways to the east of Cleveland. (Courtesy of the Western Reserve Historical Society)

These events, and most particularly the survey that followed (and would take two years), marked an epochal change in how the land and its resources were viewed. The natural markers and paths on the land, be they streams or old trails, would be subordinated to an invisible grid imposed over the entire reserve by the surveyors. They divided the land into five-mile square townships. In Cleaveland, they created a 10-acre town commons that was surrounded by smaller lots. To the east of the town lots, they laid out larger 100-acre lots suitable for farming. These stretched all the way to the border of the 5-mile Cleaveland Township. All of this was done to divide the land into a salable commodity. Only in certain areas did the lines observe the natural landscape; this occurred along the western boundary demarked by the Cuyahoga River and the northern boundary formed by the shoreline of the lake.[1]

The surveyors not only plotted the grid lines but, more importantly, assessed the potential of the land. Their notes remain key to understanding what the area looked like and what resources it held (e.g., water, trees, or good soil). The notes provide our only good view of the land as it was and as it had largely remained before full European settlement.

Particular attention was given to waterways, because they allowed the surveyors easier access to the land but more so because of the potential they would have for farmers and the resulting value of the area. When the surveyors platted out the first township, east of Cleaveland, they named it Euclid Township after the father of modern geometry. That is where they noted the brook that would soon take on the name Doan and include the highlands above the brook. Beyond the brook they found other waterways running through the forest glen, and that area would become the Village of Glenville in the next century.

Moses Cleaveland and most of the survey party returned to Connecticut in October. The survey was still incomplete, but Cleaveland told his fellow proprietors of the Connecticut Land Company that the settlement that bore his name would one day be as large as old Windham, Connecticut, at that time a community of 2,700.

When the second survey party reached Cleaveland in 1797, it was absent Moses Cleaveland but included among its workers a blacksmith, Nathaniel Doan. Doan, who was 35 years old, was in charge of the cows, oxen, and horses of the survey party. To reward him for his services (and also to spur the growth of the community), the company gave him a lot in Cleaveland. He returned home to Connecticut and in 1798 brought his wife and six children to the settlement, where he set up a blacksmith shop on Superior Street. But Doan did not stay there long. Like other early settlers, he found it difficult to endure the swarms of malarial mosquitoes that plagued the settlement. In 1799, he packed up and moved east along a trail that would come to be known as the Buffalo Road (and later Euclid Avenue). He had purchased 100 acres of land at a dollar an acre near the brook that would soon bear his surname. He built a hotel and a tavern and eventually a blacksmith shop, a store, and a saleratus factory. The area (the northwest corner of today's East 107th Street and Euclid Avenue) became known as Doan's Corners.[2]

Two aspects of the location made Doan's success possible. The first is the fact that it was close to where the road forded the brook, thus making it a good place for travelers to stop. It was also 4 miles from the city, still a considerable distance given the roads and transport at the time. The second is that the forests in the area provided

Doan Tavern as it looked in the 1930s with Melham's Market added to the front. (Courtesy of the Western Reserve Historical Society)

the basis for charcoal that he would have used in his forge before coal was available and the ashes of burnt wood that were the basis for making saleratus (potash), which was used for fertilizer and in baking (before baking soda).

Doan's settlement would eventually draw others to the western edge of Euclid Township. In 1806, Samuel Cozad Jr. purchased the land on the south side of Euclid stretching from Doan's Corners to what is today's Lake View Cemetery. His son, Samuel III, would purchase the land on the north side of the road, again stretching from Doan's Corners eastward. The Cozads would farm the land and would create a dam and a millpond on the brook at the site of today's Cleveland Museum of Art. Their home was on the site of what would be Severance Hall.

In 1837, Horatio Cyrus Ford moved from Massachusetts to the area, and he and his descendants also purchased land near Doan's Corners. He married the granddaughter of Samuel Cozad III. By the 1840s, the area now known as University Circle was the site of prosperous farms. In 1845, this section of Euclid Township would be combined with areas of two other townships to form East Cleveland[3] Township.

The community that grew in and around Euclid and Doan Brook was largely Congregational or Presbyterian and of a New England

The Cozad-Bates House was built in 1853. The house was expanded in the rear in the 1860s, and the expansion to the front was completed in 1873.

background, and its members had strong feelings about slavery. By the 1840s, the area had become one of the centers of Underground Railroad activity in Cleveland—a place where people fleeing slavery could find shelter until they were taken to Cleveland and smuggled onto a boat that took them to safety in Canada. One of the rare documents attesting to this noble, albeit risky and illegal, action can be found in the Ford and White Family Papers at the Western Reserve Historical Society. In 1846, Horatio Clark Ford (Horatio Cyrus Ford's son) made this entry in his logbook: "The two figitives [*sic*] from oppression left this morning to make their freedom sure upon the soil of Canada. I wish, in my soul, every family north of mason and Dixon&s [*sic*] line might entertain for once a panting figitive; they never would aver again, either in theory or practice, that slavery was the home of cintentment [*sic*] and righteousness."[4] Today, the Cozad-Bates House, the oldest surviving structure in the area, is home to an Underground Railroad interpretive center.

The North Union Shaker Community farm, circa 1890. (Courtesy of the Western Reserve Historical Society)

Cattle graze in the Doan Brook valley in the mid-1890s. Although the area would be transformed by the landscaping of Rockefeller Park, it had already been changed by farmers and loggers throughout the nineteenth century. (Courtesy of the Western Reserve Historical Society)

While the crossing of Euclid and Doan Brook became important, the brook's headwaters on the escarpment above became the site of a particularly unique community. In 1811, Revolutionary War veteran Jacob Russell purchased 475 acres of the upper Doan Brook valley. He and 20 family members settled in the area. But it was one of his sons, Ralph, who would change it into something special. Ralph became a member of the United Society of Believers in Christ's Second Appearing (otherwise known as the Shakers), and in 1822 he and other believers established a Shaker community on the family property. Known as the North Union Shaker Community, it was one of 19 Shaker communities established in the United States.

Founded in England by Ann Lee, the Shakers were celibate and believed in equality between genders. They became known for their

The remains of the Shaker sawmill foundation. The bench was added later by the Shaker Lakes Garden Club.

crafts, farming, music, and spirituality. The North Union Community prospered—and, one might argue, in large part because of Doan Brook. Two dams were created on branches of the brook (forming today's upper and lower Shaker lakes) to provide water for three mills: a woolen mill, a sawmill, and a large stone gristmill. By clearing the land for farming and harnessing the brook, the Shakers altered the landscape but still respected it for its beauty and productivity.[5]

By 1860, the Doan Brook watershed had evolved into a major agricultural area. The enterprise prospered not only in the upper areas with the Shakers or the area along Euclid but also in the lower reaches of its course. Along its eastern border, stretching from Euclid Avenue to the lake, one could find farms in an area that would, in 1870, be established as the Village of Glenville. Similarly, farms and settlements were growing on the western side of the brook in an area then known as East Cleveland Village, but farming was more tenuous given the rapid growth eastward of Cleveland. Although the areas along the brook were still largely pastoral, they had been significantly transformed from their original state. Farming involved the wholesale cutting of the original forest. It also brought new plant species into the area, and cattle grazing further altered the landscape and ecology of the area. And while the brook still followed its course, a series of dams had tamed its flow. All of this had occurred within less than a century.

CHAPTER 3

A PLEASANT RETREAT FROM THE CITY

As the area surrounding Doan Brook grew into a pleasant and prosperous area of farms, the city of Cleveland transformed in a different manner.

Initially envisioned as a small town that would serve a surrounding agricultural community, Cleveland became a rapidly growing mercantile center by the mid-1830s and then a nascent center of industry by the end of the Civil War. Moses Cleaveland's prediction that the settlement that then bore his name would someday be as large as old Windham, Connecticut, was finally achieved in the 1830s, the same decade that the community officially changed the spelling of its name to Cleveland.[1]

By 1820, the community numbered only 606, but 30 years later it was over 23,000 (including the population of the then separate Ohio City). In 1860, on the eve of the Civil War, the population was nearly 45,000. The growth spurt initially was made possible by water; when completed in 1832, the human-made Ohio & Erie Canal connected Cleveland on Lake Erie with Portsmouth on the Ohio River. Much of the route it followed was the same as that Native Americans had used for millennia.

The canal put Cleveland on a water transport route that started in Europe and ended at the Gulf of Mexico. It not only opened up the transport of goods produced by area farms but allowed for the easier movement of people and goods from Europe and cities on the Eastern Seaboard. The rise in business was exponential. The 1855 *Harpers Universal Gazetteer* noted, "Cleveland is the emporium of northern Ohio & next to Cincinnati, the most important town in the state."

Commerce and the creation of jobs also changed the city from a New England Protestant community to one with a more diverse population. The native-born population was joined by English, Manx, Scots, Irish, Germans, and German Jews. By 1860, 45 percent of the population was of foreign birth. Another 800 citizens were free African Americans. This growing diversity of ethnicity and religion was accommodated fairly well, but the city was not free of bias based on religion or race. Roman Catholics at times felt the sting of anti-Catholicism, but in 1847 the Catholic community was large enough to become the center of a new diocese for which a cathedral was consecrated in 1852. The Jewish community was anchored by a group of 15 German-speaking Jews from Unsleben, Bavaria, who arrived in the summer of 1839. Simpson Thorman, also from Unsleben, was in the city beforehand and led his fellow townspeople to Cleveland. He felt it had good prospects. Two years later the group established its first synagogue, Anshe Chesed (today's Fairmount Temple).[2]

The 800 free people of color who lived in the city in 1860 experienced relative tolerance, thanks in large part to the New England heritage of the city. However, they contended with state Black laws that restrained their freedom. The laws barred Blacks from voting, serving in the state militia, testifying in court against whites, and serving on juries. Until 1848, they also barred Blacks from public schools. Cleveland African Americans such as John Malvin worked to overturn the laws, and he and others worked closely with the farmers near Doan Brook as conductors on the Underground Railroad.[3]

New businesses and industry began to take over the lakefront and the areas along the Cuyahoga River in the Flats, forever altering the city's main waterway. The Flats near its mouth became a warren of warehouses and wholesale brokers, one of whom was a young John D. Rockefeller. He eventually would deal in petroleum and build a refinery in 1863 at the site where Kingsbury Run flowed into the Cuyahoga. It became a convenient sewer for unusable byproducts, including, at that time, gasoline. Five years later, in 1868, waste products from the refinery caught fire on the Cuyahoga River; it was a mere 72 years after the first settlement of the city. Debris on the surface of the river would continue to combust for another century.

Once almost totally centered in the area west of Public Square, Cleveland expanded toward the south along Pittsburgh and Broadway Roads. Formerly prime residential areas west of Public Square became less desirable as business and industry grew—as did pollution. The population, in large part, moved to the east of Public Square. In 1872, the portion of East Cleveland (formerly Euclid) Township running east from Willson Avenue (now East Fifty-Fifth) was annexed. Hough Avenue, running eastward from Willson, was dedicated the following year. What had been the farmland of Oliver and Eliza Hough became a subdivision of building lots soon to be filled with substantial middle-class and upper-middle-class homes. By the late 1880s, residences were abutting the Doan Brook valley in some areas.

The wealthiest members of the community also, in large part, moved eastward. However, they chose to display their good fortune in very large homes, the biggest of which were situated on Euclid Avenue. It eventually became known as Millionaire's Row. Euclid in some ways mimicked the main streets in smaller towns wherein homes of the well-to-do were constructed on the main street just beyond the business district. But it was far grander, and as the city grew, the mansions did as well and also began to stretch out eastward along Euclid. By the early 1880s, they had reached Willson Avenue and soon would stretch even farther eastward.

Among those who could afford a Euclid address was Jeptha Homer Wade. Born into a farm family in the Finger Lakes area of New York, he was a self-made man. He was apprenticed as a tanner, worked as a carpenter and joiner, held a position in a window sash and blind factory, became an itinerant portrait painter (one of his paintings is in the Cleveland Museum of Art), and then worked as a contractor building telegraph lines. He would eventually become one of the founders of Western Union Telegraph. In the summer of 1856, he and his family settled in Cleveland where he and his son, Randall, built side-by-side mansions on Euclid at the northwest corner of what is now East Fortieth Street. Like other wealthy

Jeptha Homer Wade I, with his son Jeptha Homer Wade II ("Homer") and his grandson Jeptha Homer Wade III. The Wade family played a critical role in the evolution of the lower Doan Brook valley. (Courtesy of the Western Reserve Historical Society)

Clevelanders, Wade also desired something a bit more pastoral, and he looked eastward to the area of Doan Brook and the escarpment above it for that country retreat.

In 1872, Wade purchased a large section of the Cozad farm north of Euclid Avenue and began landscaping it as a private park. His familiarity with the area had already been established when he, Joseph Perkins, and Henry B. Payne led the establishment of a new cemetery. After looking at sites along the lakeshore, they opted instead for the edge of the Portage Escarpment along Euclid Avenue. There they established Lake View Cemetery, through which a branch of Dugway Brook ran, down from the escarpment edge on the road to Mayfield Township to the old lake floor at the northern edge of the cemetery. All of this was just to the east of the park that, when completed, Wade opened to the public on weekends. In 1882, he donated more than 63 acres of his landscaped rural getaway running north from Euclid along Doan Brook to the city of Cleveland for use as a public park.[4]

Initially, the city had qualms about accepting the gift. Some officials felt it was too far away from the center of the population to be fully accessible to the public. Another complaint was the cost of maintaining it. Fortunately, the city accepted the gift. Wade Park would arguably be the key to everything that followed regarding the public use of the Doan Brook watershed.

Wade's private park was not the first along the brook. At its mouth on Lake Erie, another private park took shape. William J. Gordon, who had made a fortune in wholesale groceries and the iron ore business, began buying land around the mouth of Doan Brook on the shore of Lake Erie in 1865 for a private park. He eventually accumulated 122 acres and, like Wade, landscaped it. It was bequeathed to the city upon Gordon's death in 1892. Its lakeside location, similar to that of Perkins Beach and Edgewater Park (which were west of the Cuyahoga River and were purchased by the city in 1894 from Jacob B. Perkins), eventually provided bathing beaches for the citizens. Each was located far enough away from the mouth of the Cuyahoga River to avoid the pollutants that flowed constantly from that waterway.[5]

At the same time, other wealthy Clevelanders began to look at the top of the escarpment as a getaway from the city. Dr. Nathan Hardy Ambler, a dentist who had made a small fortune during the

California Gold Rush by being paid in gold for his dental work, bought land on the escarpment in 1872 around the route of Doan Brook. He built a mansion for himself and later made another fortune selling real estate in the area.

Also drawn to the heights was John D. Rockefeller, who bought land farther east on the escarpment around one of the branches of Dugway Brook. He planned with a group of investors to create a "water cure and place of public resort." That failed, but the completed

The beach at Gordon Park, circa 1910. (Courtesy of the Western Reserve Historical Society)

In the late 1910s, the landscape of Gordon Park was a handsome complement to its bathing beach. (Courtesy of the Western Reserve Historical Society)

Surveyors work on plotting out the parkway road to Ambler Heights in the 1890s. (Courtesy of the Western Reserve Historical Society)

structure became his second home (his other was on Euclid Avenue across the street from the Wades). When he took up residence in New York City in 1884, Forest Hill (in what is now East Cleveland and Cleveland Heights) became his summer retreat. Eventually, he would purchase 700 acres in the area.[6]

Wade Park, in particular, helped set up another major change in the area of Doan's Corners. In 1882, Amasa Stone, who had built his fortune in building and running railroads, donated $500,000 to underwrite the move of Western Reserve College from Hudson, Ohio, to Cleveland. This donation came with a proviso that included clauses that citizens donate money for the land and that the site also house the Case School of Applied Science (established in 1880 by a bequest from Leonard Case Jr.). The local citizenry came through, purchasing farmland and orchards on the north side of Euclid just east of Doan Brook that were owned by Liberty Holden and Martha Cordelia Cozad Ford. By 1884, both schools had relocated and added another important dimension to the Doan Brook watershed—a center of higher education.[7]

By the 1890s, Wade Park was a popular destination for Clevelanders and was no longer a farming community. Accessible by electric streetcar from the city, it was relatively easy to reach, and the turning circle for the streetcars along with the universities provided the area with a name, University Circle. New institutions arrived in the area during that decade, among them the Western Reserve Historical Society, which moved from Public Square to a new building in 1898 at what is now Euclid Avenue and Stokes Boulevard. And, at the same time, the area around what is now Euclid and East 105th Street was developing into a commercial center that would in a decade or two be considered Cleveland's second downtown.

The Centaur Fountain was the central feature in the Wade Park Lagoon. This picture shows the lagoon circa 1888, with a boathouse and two young visitors. (Courtesy of the Western Reserve Historical Society)

This view of Doan Brook and its valley in the mid-1890s provides a sense of what the area looked like before the creation of Rockefeller Park. (Courtesy of the Western Reserve Historical Society)

Certainly, the city had come to appreciate parks, because by the early 1880s its newly created Park Board had purchased the first 89 acres of Edgewater Park from Joseph Perkins and also 81 acres that would become Brookside Park on the city's west side. However, after Gordon's bequest in 1892, the most obvious task for the board was to close the gap between Wade Park and Gordon Park. As a contiguous park, it would link University Circle with the lakefront and provide the city with a grand parkway from its growing cultural center to the lake. Images of it from the period show it as a still quasi-rural shamble of pastures and trees.

The Park Board purchased a significant segment of the land. Its acquisition was part of a larger plan to encircle the city with parks connected by broad boulevards, a plan for which the board had hired Ernest W. Bowditch, a noted landscape architect from Boston. Bowditch had immense experience in landscaping and landscape architecture. He had worked with Frederick Olmsted Sr. and John Charles Olmsted. Frederick Olmsted had created both

Boston's Emerald Necklace and New York's Central Park, two icons of park design in that century.[8]

Getting the remaining lands to create the lower Doan Brook park was critical, particularly after the Shaker Land Company donated 279 acres encompassing the upper watershed of Doan Brook and the two Shaker lakes to the city in 1895. This had been part of the Shaker community, which had dissolved in 1889 and its land then purchased for real estate speculation. So, the community had before it the chance to rescue a good portion of the Doan Brook watershed (such as it was at that time—dammed in several areas and partially bridged and, at places, hidden in culverts in the University Circle area).

The news that the project would be fully funded and completed was announced as a surprise at an event commemorating the city's centennial in 1896. John D. Rockefeller had sent an announcement that he would purchase 276 acres along the watershed and donate $300,000 to the city to cover the costs already expended on land acquisition. Wade Park and Gordon Park would now be linked by Rockefeller Park, ensuring the protection of the lower watershed.[9]

In a way, this was a mixed blessing, because the creation of the park would change the valley. Much of what remained of the edges of the original watershed were landscaped—sculpted with embankments and planted with grass and trees not necessarily indigenous to the area. Doan Brook was channeled in places to prevent erosion. A new lake, for boating and ice skating, was created at the south end of the park, and a scenic lower drive wound its way through the valley. It was not an original landscape, yet it became a new landscape dedicated to natural beauty, relaxation, and pleasure. Four magnificent bridges designed by the city's leading architect, Charles F. Schweinfurth, carried three major streets and the Lake Shore & Michigan Southern Railroad safely and beautifully over Doan Brook and the lower drive. It was a stunning transformation, but only the brook remained to speak vaguely of its history.[10]

Above the valley's embankments, along the drive, under the escarpment, and hugging the edge of the university campus were new residents, ones whose presence spoke of major changes in the community. New immigrant groups, largely from central, southern, and eastern Europe, had come to Cleveland to work in its growing industrial economy. St. Clair Avenue was beginning to fill with Slovenes,

The St. Clair Avenue bridge is the first of four bridges designed and built by Charles F. Schweinfurth over the Doan Brook valley between 1897 and 1900.

The Wade Park Avenue bridge is the second Charles F. Schweinfurth bridge to be built over the Doan Brook valley.

The Superior Avenue bridge is the third Charles F. Schweinfurth bridge to be built over the Doan Brook valley.

The Lake Shore & Michigan Southern (now Conrail) Railroad bridge is the final Charles F. Schweinfurth bridge to be built over the Doan Brook valley.

Above: Skating at the Rockefeller Park Lagoon in the early 1900s. (Courtesy of the Western Reserve Historical Society)

Right: This image shows Rockefeller Park shortly after it was completed with Lower Drive, Doan Brook, and newly planted trees. (Courtesy of the Western Reserve Historical Society)

Left: The Wade Park Avenue bridge is, perhaps, the most elegant of the four bridges designed for Rockefeller Park by noted Cleveland architect Charles F. Schweinfurth. This image shows it under construction in the late 1890s. (Courtesy of the Western Reserve Historical Society)

Above: A summer view with boaters on the lagoon in Rockefeller Park. (Courtesy of the Western Reserve Historical Society)

Serbs, and Croatians, and Mayfield Road became the center of a community known as Little Italy. By 1900, Cleveland's population had grown to nearly 382,000, nearly a third of which was of foreign birth. At the same time in Boston, there were new designs afoot—not ones to reshape the land but to reconstruct the laws governing who might be allowed to come to the United States. Those designs would eventually be challenged in the parkland along Doan Brook.

CHAPTER 4

CREATING A PLACE TO REMEMBER

In August 1905, William P. Palmer, a steel mill executive and son of a Civil War veteran, sent a letter to Mayor Tom L. Johnson of Cleveland. Palmer, who lived in a grand house on Overlook Road in the new village of Cleveland Heights, was upset with the fireworks set off by the Italians who lived in Little Italy, just below his home on the edge of the escarpment. The fireworks were an important component of the Feast of the Assumption celebration, part of the culture the Italians had brought with them to Cleveland. Johnson punted and sent the letter to his police chief, who told Palmer that there was nothing he could do because the fireworks were set off beyond the city's boundaries.[1]

This story was, in a general sense, not unique. As immigrants continued to come into Cleveland, older residents moved away. Many like Palmer chose the heights, an area above the pollution in the city and apart from its demographic changes. As Cleveland Heights developed, it signified what image it intended by choosing street names that reflected English places—Berkshire, Yorkshire, Coventry, and Hampshire. Architectural styles were also often Anglophilic. It was not Little Italy.

Shaker Heights, which was developed by Oris Paxton and Mantis James Van Sweringen beginning in 1905, echoed these sentiments. A "garden city" suburb, it carefully controlled the styles

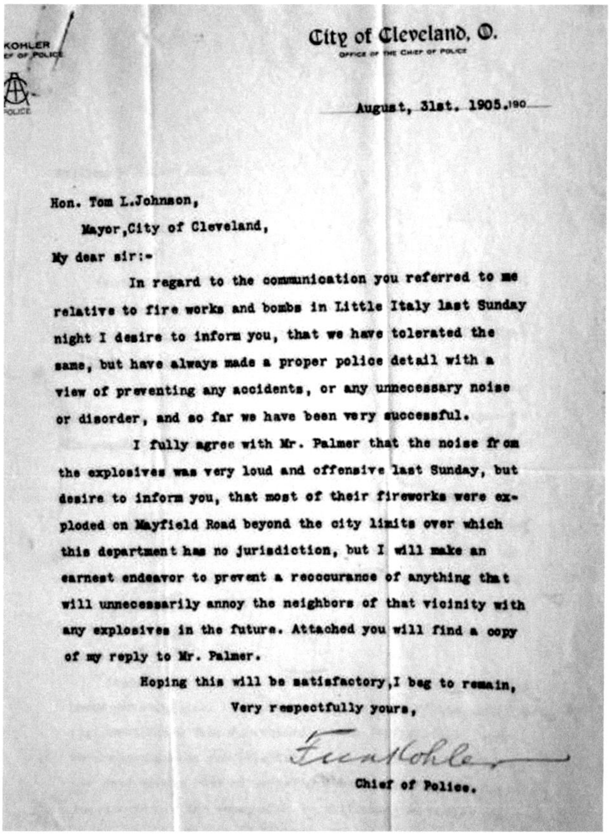

KOHLER
CHIEF OF POLICE

City of Cleveland, O.
OFFICE OF THE CHIEF OF POLICE

August, 31st. 1905.

Hon. Tom L.Johnson,
Mayor,City of Cleveland,

My dear sir:-

In regard to the communication you referred to me relative to fire works and bombs in Little Italy last Sunday night I desire to inform you, that we have tolerated the same, but have always made a proper police detail with a view of preventing any accidents, or any unnecessary noise or disorder, and so far we have been very successful.

I fully agree with Mr. Palmer that the noise from the explosives was very loud and offensive last Sunday, but desire to inform you, that most of their fireworks were exploded on Mayfield Road beyond the city limits over which this department has no jurisdiction, but I will make an earnest endeavor to prevent a reoccurance of anything that will unnecessarily annoy the neighbors of that vicinity with any explosives in the future. Attached you will find a copy of my reply to Mr. Palmer.

Hoping this will be satisfactory,I beg to remain,
Very respectfully yours,

Fred Kohler
Chief of Police.

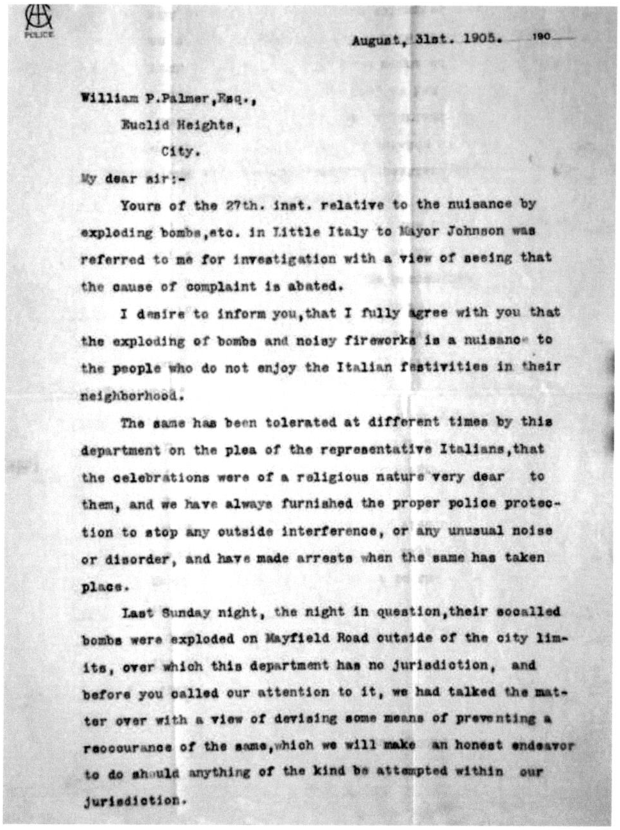

POLICE

August, 31st. 1905.

William P.Palmer,Esq.,
Euclid Heights,
City.

My dear sir:-

Yours of the 27th. inst. relative to the nuisance by exploding bombs,etc. in Little Italy to Mayor Johnson was referred to me for investigation with a view of seeing that the cause of complaint is abated.

I desire to inform you,that I fully agree with you that the exploding of bombs and noisy fireworks is a nuisance to the people who do not enjoy the Italian festivities in their neighborhood.

The same has been tolerated at different times by this department on the plea of the representative Italians,that the celebrations were of a religious nature very dear to them, and we have always furnished the proper police protection to stop any outside interference, or any unusual noise or disorder, and have made arrests when the same has taken place.

Last Sunday night, the night in question,their socalled bombs were exploded on Mayfield Road outside of the city limits, over which this department has no jurisdiction, and before you called our attention to it, we had talked the matter over with a view of devising some means of preventing a reoccurance of the same,which we will make an honest endeavor to do should anything of the kind be attempted within our jurisdiction.

These letters, from Cleveland police chief Frederica Kohler, relate to a complaint by a resident on Overlook Road of Cleveland Heights, William P. Palmer, about the fireworks being used in Little Italy by the Italians who lived "down the hill" from him. (Courtesy of the Western Reserve Historical Society)

and colors of the homes built there. More critically, it imposed restrictive covenants, in which homeowners on a street needed to approve any new purchases. That effectively kept Jews and African Americans out of the area for decades to come.[2]

Nevertheless, while this was occurring, the new immigrants coming into the city were quick to continue their own cultural traditions—like the festive fireworks in Little Italy that troubled William Palmer. Indeed, the churches and synagogues the immigrants built were bastions of ethnic identity; they served as the new communities' first cultural monuments. Even more remarkable was the creation of monuments and statues in public venues that reflected on a particular culture. In creating these monuments, the new immigrants were following a long local tradition.

The first public monument erected in the city was a statue of Oliver Hazard Perry, who led the American naval victory at the Battle of Lake Erie in September 1813. That engagement was, indeed, critical to the fortunes of Cleveland. Had the British prevailed in that battle and the war, the settlement and much of the Northwest

The Perry Monument in the center of Public Square (which was fenced at this time), circa 1865. (Courtesy of the Western Reserve Historical Society)

Territory might have fallen under British control. The Perry Monument was dedicated on September 10, 1860—the anniversary date of the battle—and was situated at the center of the intersection of Superior and Ontario Streets in the exact middle of Public Square. Public Square, or the town commons, was another symbol of the city's roots as it mirrored a New England tradition. With its Protestant church and a courthouse, it reflected the first dominant European culture to inhabit the area—it was, and it remains today, a monument onto itself.

However, that tradition was complemented by the celebrations held by newer immigrant groups. The Irish held their first St. Patrick's Day parade in 1842. It was a small affair near the first Catholic Church in Cleveland, St. Mary's on the Flats, but over the years it would grow larger and become a staple of the city's annual celebrations, taking over much of the city's downtown.

Crowds gather at the arch on Public Square to celebrate the Franco-Prussian War Peace Jubilee in April 1871. (Courtesy of the Western Reserve Historical Society)

Then in 1871, a new, albeit temporary, monument was erected on Public Square. It was a triumphal arch celebrating the Prussian victory in the recent Franco-Prussian War, a victory that brought about the creation of the German Empire. Erected by the city's large German-speaking community, it reflected their pride in the homeland. Rev. Dr. Jacob Myer, the leader of the German Jewish congregation Tifereth Israel (today's Temple), served as president of the planning committee and gave one of the main addresses at the celebration. The parade that flowed through Public Square and under the arch took 58 minutes to pass.[3]

In the 1880s, public memory changed again as the immense Soldiers' and Sailors' Monument was erected, after much contention, on the square. Dedicated on July 4, 1884, it commemorated the contributions made by area soldiers and citizens in the Civil War.

It remains one of the largest Civil War monuments in the nation. The contention that surrounded its erection was largely centered on the issue of public memory. Its proposed position on the southeast quadrant of the square would replace the Perry Monument (which had been moved there from its original position some years before). The Civil War won, and Perry lost. His monument moved to a new position in Wade Park, and by doing so it seems to have set a precedent.[4]

In 1902, the Hungarian community sought permission to erect a monument to its national hero, Louis Kossuth, on Public Square. It was to celebrate the fiftieth anniversary of Kossuth's visit to the United States and Cleveland. As an advocate for the independence of Hungary, Kossuth was a very popular figure in the United States—indeed, a symbol of liberty. Mayor Tom Johnson initially approved the plan but then ran into a wave of opposition. The opposition was led by the Slovak community, which, at that time, lived in and had come from the Hungarian section of the Austro-Hungarian Empire. It viewed the Magyars, and Kossuth, as oppressors of Slovak culture and freedom. This was an early instance of public administrative ignorance of ethnic issues. The Slovaks in Cleveland quickly built a coalition of other Slavic groups in the city—the first instance when separate groups of recent immigrants had united for a cause. Members of the coalition approached the mayor. Their argument was clever; they subordinated their grievances to something more politically practical. They noted that if the city placed a monument to one ethnic community on the square, it would eventually have to accommodate other communities. Mayor Johnson had come to fully understand the real politics behind their objection and possibly the argument they presented to him. He rescinded the earlier decision. Instead, the Hungarian community was given a new site—next to the streetcar turning circle in University Circle—directly across the street from Wade Park.[5]

The Perry Monument in Wade Park. The monument was removed from Public Square in 1892 and then relocated to the park in 1894. (Courtesy of the Western Reserve Historical Society)

Three years later, the Polish community also celebrated its contribution to liberty by erecting a statue of Thaddeus Kosciuszko, a Polish army officer and statesman who had helped the colonies win the American Revolution. Like that of Kossuth, the statue had a double meaning because Kosciusko was also a potent symbol of freedom in their homeland, which at the time remained divided among Germany, Austria-Hungary, and Russia. It was also erected

A large crowd gathers to celebrate the dedication of the Louis Kossuth Monument in University Circle in 1902. (Courtesy of the Western Reserve Historical Society)

in University Circle, placed directly in Wade Park at a site (where it still stands) just to the west of where the Cleveland Museum of Art would be built. Why the Poles of Cleveland decided to erect the statue at this time is still not fully clear. As a statement of Poland's contribution to the cause of American freedom, it may also have served as an antidote to growing moves to limit immigration. Cleveland's Poles also had the memory of the recent assassination of President William McKinley in 1901, an act carried out by Leon Czolgosz, a Clevelander and the son of Polish immigrants. Within the Polish community itself, there was a vigorous debate about the monument. Some contended that Kosciuszko's face was molded after one of the sponsors of the project, Father Anton Kolaszewski, a former pastor of St. Stanislaus Church whose tenure there had split the community into two factions.[6] The story of the creation of the Kossuth and Kosciusko statues also referenced a factor of which the general community was unaware—the factions and fractures within groups. These have continued to the present day.

In 1904, Cleveland's Polish community erected this statue of Thaddeus Kosciuszko, who served as a colonel in the Continental army during the American Revolution, in Wade Park. (Courtesy of the Western Reserve Historical Society)

In 1907, another immigrant monument was dedicated in Wade Park. In this instance, the German community of Cleveland raised the money for an exact copy of the Goethe-Schiller Monument that had been erected in Weimar in 1847. It was one of four copies erected or to be erected in the United States; the others were in San Francisco in 1901, Milwaukee in 1908, and Syracuse in 1911. This was a time during which German culture—poetry, literature, science, and music—was at the forefront in the United States and a time when the German American community was highly respected and active in business and civic affairs. In Cleveland, it was also a time when

The Goethe-Schiller Monument was dedicated in Wade Park in 1907. (Courtesy of the Western Reserve Historical Society)

some Germans were worried that the community was assimilating too rapidly into the new American culture—and thus the monument was a reminder of a deep cultural heritage, one that was recognized inside and outside of the German community. Sixty-five thousand people turned out for the monument's dedication.

Shortly after World War I, in 1922, a fourth "ethnic" monument would appear in Wade Park when the Cleveland Slovak Community dedicated a monument to General Milan R. Stefanik, an aviator, soldier, and advocate for the creation of a Czechoslovak state. Erected at the intersection of Jeptha Drive with East Boulevard, it stood just below the relatively new Cleveland Museum of Art.

These four monuments not only reflected the power of and internal issues within the groups that created an increasingly diverse city, but they also provided a prelude of sorts to the creation of the Cultural Gardens. Indeed, the Goethe-Schiller Monument would be moved to the gardens and eventually also would the Stefanik statue. Yet each was created at a time when open immigration to the United States was being challenged.

Until 1882, immigration to the United States was not encumbered by a myriad of legalities; there were no visas necessary and no quotas. Essentially, one booked passage and came. Up to that year, individual states with ports governed incoming immigrants. For a long time, however, there had been legal arguments that the federal government needed to oversee the process. One factor related to the fact that cities and states had been collecting money from incoming vessels to offset possible welfare costs associated with new arrivals: essentially, it was a tax placed on international commerce. This was eventually ruled as invalid, as the Constitution had assigned the role of overseeing and taxing international commerce to the federal government.

When the federal government finally assumed the responsibility in 1882, it barred the entrance of individuals likely to be a public charge and those with loathsome or contagious diseases. In a move directed at incoming Mormon converts, it also banned those practicing polygamy. In that same year, the United States also passed the Chinese Exclusion Act, the first law to ban an entire category of immigrants based on their ethnicity or race. Its restrictions would last until 1943.

As the patterns of immigration shifted away from northern and western Europe, others began to seek a means to limit emigration from these newer areas. This, too, was based on the racial theories of the time, theories that argued that individuals from southern, central, and eastern Europe were inferior to those from northern and western parts of the continent. In 1894, three Harvard College graduates, Charles Warren, Robert DeCourcy Ward, and Prescott Farnsworth Hall, founded the Immigration Restriction League. The league's stated purpose was to exclude "elements undesirable for citizenship or injurious to our national character." This related directly to the growing numbers of Jews, Italians, Greeks, and South Slavs coming to the United States.

It proposed to achieve this goal by having Congress pass a law banning the immigration of people (i.e., family heads and children over 16 years of age) who were not literate in their own language. The literacy test was based on the assumption that this would not affect emigrants from northern or western Europe but would instead stifle the flow from southern, eastern, and central Europe.

The campaign for the legislation attracted many intellectual leaders, some of whom were deeply caught up in the racial theories of the time as well as eugenics; however, it was problematic for the businesses and industries that depended on a flow of cheap immigrant labor. It was voted on by Congress at least five times between

1897 and 1915, and each time it either failed or was vetoed by the president. Then, in the hyper-patriotic period of World War I, it was passed by Congress and vetoed by President Woodrow Wilson, but Congress had the votes to override his veto and pass the legislation. It was just the beginning of a process to control immigration on a racialized basis.[7]

The changes occurring in the city's overall population were not simply created by immigration but also by migration from within the United States. It was at and after the turn of the century that the city saw growing arrivals of African Americans fleeing the South as part of the first Great Migration. In 1880, the city's Black population stood slightly over 2,000; by 1910, it had risen to over 8,400; and by 1920, it had grown to 34,451. The growth of the local Black community came at a time when attitudes toward race in the American North, even in cities like Cleveland that had been fairly integrated, hardened. As the Black population increased, it was confined largely to one area stretching along Cedar Avenue from the center city to ultimately University Circle. Public accommodations and amusement parks, such as Luna Park and Euclid Beach, began discriminatory practices. To its credit, the city government often intervened, but the problem continued. George Myers, an African American who came to Cleveland from Maryland in 1879, had experiences that reflected these changes. He was a barber and eventually operated the barbershop in Hollenden Hotel, which was *the* hotel in Cleveland, particularly for politicians. A loyal Republican, he helped garner votes for Marcus Hanna's senatorial campaign and William McKinley's presidential runs. He also was a frequent correspondent with noted historian James Ford Rhodes, a brother-in-law of Hanna. His correspondence with Rhodes reflects his loyalty to the Republican Party but also, as time went on, his increasing frustration with changes he saw around him as prejudice increased in the city. For a while, his barbershop remained a mecca for Black employment with 35 workers. In 1923, the management of the hotel told him that upon his retirement, all Black barbers would be replaced with white employees. He died in 1930 at the ticket window of the railroad station while planning his travel upon retirement.[8]

The growth of the Black population—motivated by Jim Crow laws, lynching, and the lack of opportunities in the South—was further catalyzed by the outbreak of World War I. Well before the entry of the United States into the conflict in April 1917, American businesses and industries began producing war goods for Britain and its allies. American factories needed more labor than ever, but the flow of people from Europe was interrupted by the war. The need was met largely by internal migrations. The conflict not only shifted migration patterns, but it also tested the relationships between ethnic groups that had come from the combatant nations in cities such as Cleveland. Once America entered the war, many of its citizens would question the loyalty of Germans and those groups allied with them.

Although opinion about who was right and who was wrong in the new European war was divided in Cleveland in the early months of the conflict, it began to shift after the sinking of the *Lusitania* in May 1915—and because of a barrage of Allied propaganda. Sides were slowly taken, but by 1916 one could argue that Cleveland had sided with the Allies. Two events, a movie and the creation of a prototype for the Cultural Gardens, provide some insight into this.

The movie was *The Perils of Society,* a somewhat comic melodrama inspired, perhaps, by the *Perils of Pauline* series. It was acted out by members of Cleveland's upper crust at all their favorite venues, including the Union Club, the Country Club, and fox hunting in the Chagrin Valley. It was filmed by Katherine Bleeker, considered one of the first female cranks—or filmmakers. The purpose was twofold: to have fun and, more important, to support a war-related charitable effort. Premiering in June 1916 at the Metropolitan Theater (today's Agora) on Euclid Avenue, its purpose was to raise funds for the support of French war orphans.

The second event took place on April 14, 1916, to honor the three hundredth anniversary of the death of William Shakespeare. It was arguably the beginning of Cleveland's Cultural Gardens. It came about at the suggestion of Leo Weidenthal. Born in Cleveland on April 23, 1878 (the same month and day of Shakespeare's birth), Weidenthal established a long career as a newspaperman working as a reporter for three dailies. Later in his career, he cofounded the Cleveland chapter of the National Conference of Christians and Jews. But his real love was the theater, and, upon his death, he left an enormous body of material on the topic to the Cleveland Public Library.[9]

That love of the theater and his date of birth put him on Cleveland's committee for the commemoration of the tercentenary of Shakespeare's death, and it was his suggestion that part of the memorial event involve the creation of a Shakespeare garden. The committee and the city agreed, and a plot of land located on East Boulevard, just above the east side of the Doan Brook valley in Rockefeller Park, was set aside for it. It took the shape of a typical Elizabethan garden, and its plantings included daisies, maples, sycamore, roses, and ivy—all of which were typical of a seventeenth-century English garden. Some of the plants were from local collections, and others came from England. The dedication ceremony included comments by mayor Harry Davis and readings of Shakespeare's sonnets by noted actress Julia Marlow. Guests were formally seated and guided to their places by young students dressed in Elizabethan costume. Later, other notable guests, including writers such as Rabindranath Tagore (the "Shakespeare of India") and figures from the theatrical world, visited the garden, helping it gain a reputation as a place of poetry, culture, and beauty. A poet's corner for readings became an important part of the site.

Whether purposeful, the Shakespeare Garden and the tercentenary were reminders of America's link to Great Britain and to its mother tongue. And when the United States entered the war one year after its dedication, concerns grew about those who were not yet American and those whose loyalties might be compromised by their heritage.

Those who were German or of German descent found themselves and their language, music, and culture targeted by the patriotism of the time. There were 134,000 citizens of German extraction in the city at that time. Much of German communal life would die out during the war, when the once-common study of German in the public schools came almost to an end. The German American president of Baldwin Wallace College found himself suspended after allowing the Christmas carol "Silent Night" to be sung in its original language. And for those not of German background, the movement to Americanize immigrants, which had begun nationally in earnest in the 1890s, accelerated.[10]

Cleveland quickly established the Mayor's Advisory War Committee to help chart the city's path through the war. Its duties included dealing with matters such as war production, rationing,

The Shakespeare Garden, dedicated on April 14, 1916, honoring the poet's death 300 years earlier. The garden would become known as the British Garden in 1934.

Facing page: Here is the sign explaining the oak trees lining the nine-mile length of Liberty Boulevard (now Martin Luther King Jr. Boulevard) and North Park Boulevard to the entrance of the upper Shaker lakes. Dedicated May 30, 1919.

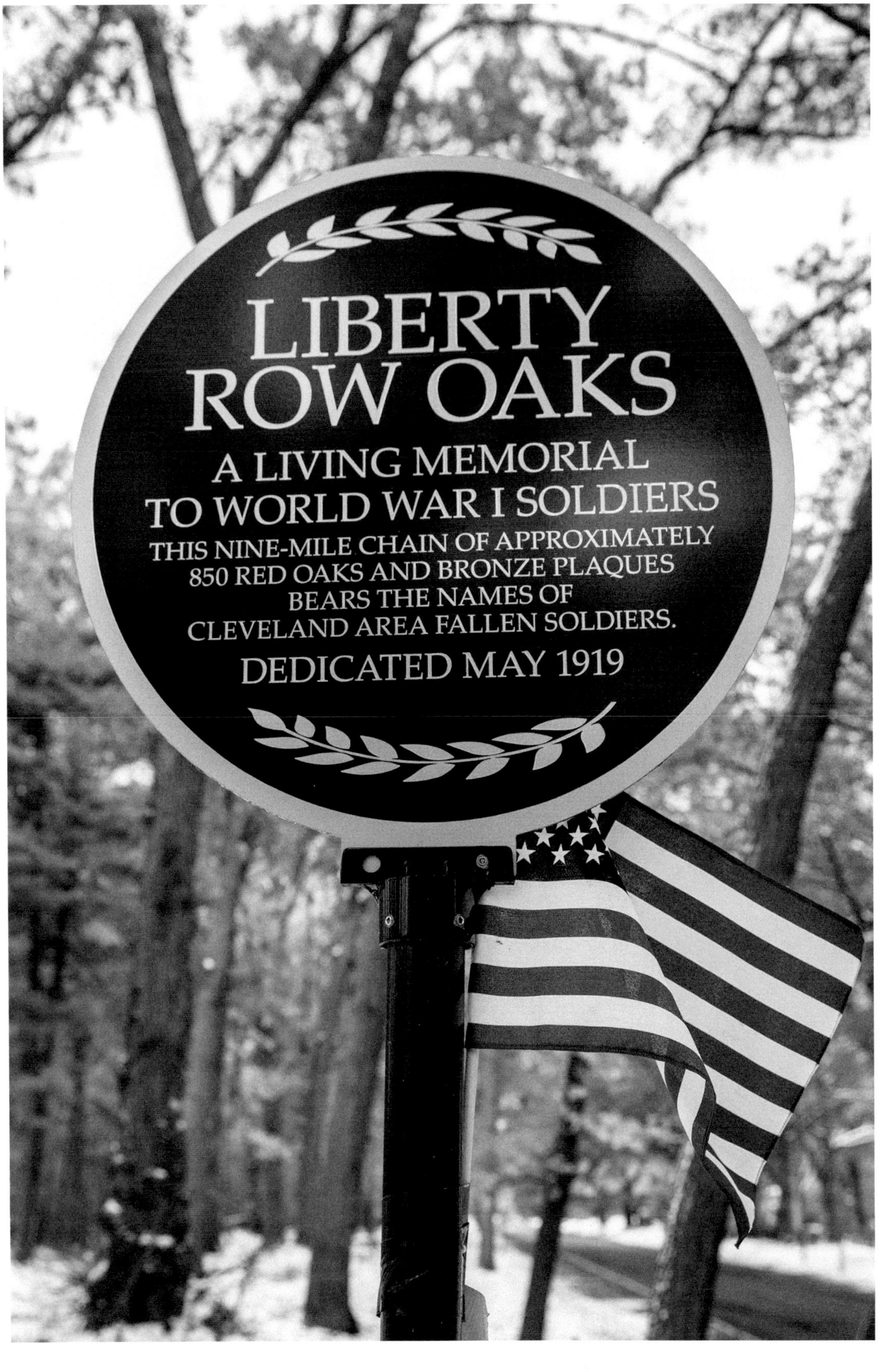
LIBERTY
ROW OAKS
A LIVING MEMORIAL
TO WORLD WAR I SOLDIERS
THIS NINE-MILE CHAIN OF APPROXIMATELY
850 RED OAKS AND BRONZE PLAQUES
BEARS THE NAMES OF
CLEVELAND AREA FALLEN SOLDIERS.
DEDICATED MAY 1919

Bronze plaques, each bearing the name of one of Cleveland's fallen warriors, were installed at the foot of each tree of the Liberty Row Oaks. Dedicated May 30, 1919.

raising funds to support the war effort, and building a unified city. It quickly assembled an Americanization committee comprised of leading figures from many of the city's ethnic groups who the members of the advisory committee believed could best reach the Poles, Slovaks, Italians, and other immigrant communities. This pattern of selecting the *promeneti* of a particular community for civic service

The effort to Americanize Cleveland's immigrant population accelerated during the nation's involvement in World War I. This poster encourages young children to have their parents learn English in the public schools. (Courtesy of the Western Reserve Historical Society)

would have a long life and would, indeed, color the creation of the Cultural Gardens.[11] The committee focused on promoting Americanization, particularly the study of English. One of the posters it issued was titled "Many People: One Language." Printed with a message in six languages, its graphic content encouraged schoolchildren to encourage their immigrant parents to go to special classes to learn English. Importantly, the committee also produced what were the first historical studies of major immigrant groups in the city—this in an attempt to help the community better understand its diversity. It published seven booklets detailing the histories of the Polish, Czech, Slovak, Italian, Hungarian, Lithuanian, and Jugoslav communities. They remain today as valuable resources for understanding these groups at a particular time. But each, in its own way, stretched a bit in trying to connect a group's national history to the struggle for democracy.

When the war ended in November 1918, the city began a slow movement back to normalcy. It had lost 1,023 men in battle or to sickness while in the armed forces. It has also produced $750 million worth of munitions during the four years of the war. And, after the war, it confronted labor strife (including the May Day Riot in 1919 that took the lives of two) and, over time, increasing questions about the validity of American participation in the war.[12]

Yet the city had to find a way to remember those who gave their lives. It decided to dedicate much of the Doan Brook watershed to their memories. It did so in 1919 by renaming the lower drive Liberty Boulevard and then by planting an oak tree for each of the fallen. The trees, each accompanied by a bronze marker with the name of someone who had died while in service, stretched beyond the lower watershed into Shaker Heights, following the course of Doan Brook for the entire route. The Doan Brook valley had now fully assumed a new identity: as a memorial to the fallen. However, the Shakespeare Garden posited another potential identity, one that would come into full form in the mid-1920s.

CHAPTER 5

EQUALITIES OF CULTURES

On November 10, 1921, Marshall Ferdinand Foch of France, the supreme Allied commander during World War I, visited Cleveland. His appearance in Cleveland was part of a 3,000-mile circuit of visits to major cities in the United States. He got off his private train car at the East 105th Street station near Bratenahl. From there, he proceeded westward along Lakeshore Boulevard with a cortege of cars that was accompanied by members of Cleveland's Troop A, a cavalry unit. Troop A had seen action in the war but had its origins as a local militia created in the 1870s by a number of well-to-do citizens to confront potential labor violence.[1]

According to the news coverage of the time, the cortege turned to go south on the lower boulevard (Liberty Boulevard) and traveled to University Circle. One wonders what was said to Foch as they traveled along the newly dedicated memorial. Certainly something. After a very long day in Cleveland, he returned to the station and set off for his next stop in Pittsburgh.

Foch was but one of the dignitaries who in the 1920s entered Cleveland by this route. At that point in time, it was, perhaps, better for someone traveling by train to exit at the East 105th Street station rather than continue (as some did) to the old, decrepit Union Station at the foot of West Ninth Street on the lakefront. And Liberty Boulevard was a convenient access route to University Circle and then, via Euclid Avenue, to the center of the city. The boulevard was indeed a showpiece for the city—a landscaped green space amid the neighborhoods and industries that had overwhelmed what had been open farmland.

By 1920, Cleveland was the nation's fifth-largest city and the value of its industrial production also ranked fifth in the nation. Two-thirds of its population had been born abroad or were the children of immigrants, and another 35,000 were African American. It was not so much a melting pot as it was a patchwork of neighborhoods defined by one's nationality, ethnicity, or race. If Foch's entourage had chosen to drive south along East 105th street through what had been Glenville, he would have encountered a large Jewish community. If he had left the boulevard and traveled west via St. Clair, he would have seen a vast industrial area populated by Slovenes, Poles, Serbs, and Croats. And, if rather than taking Euclid west toward downtown, the entourage had selected Cedar Avenue, he would have been in the midst of a growing Black community. Essentially, the Doan Brook watershed, from Shaker Heights to the lake, was a place "apart" from the city but still accessible to all. Indeed, some who lived alongside the lower drives would sleep out on its lawns on hot summer nights.

Yet 1921, the year that Foch visited the city, was also the year that the United States initiated an overall limitation of immigration that would remain in place until 1965. The Emergency Quota Act of 1921 set a numerical limit (350,000) on emigration from the Eastern Hemisphere, with quotas that favored groups from northern and western European states. The quotas were based on the number of each nationality represented in the 1910 census—only 3 percent of the total population of each group would be allowed entry. It came about largely because of an increase of immigrants fleeing the chaos and destruction of postwar Europe and because the Literacy Act of 1917 was a failure (immigrants were more literate than expected). However, one part of the 1917 act remained in place: the creation of the Asiatic Barred Zone Act that prevented most emigration from an area stretching from Turkey eastward to New Guinea.

The emergency act created chaos for shipping companies and immigrants who now needed visas to enter. However, it did not accomplish the task at its core—to stanch large-scale emigration from eastern Europe. It was replaced by a new permanent quota law, the

Johnson-Reed Act in 1924, which set a limit of 165,000 immigrants per year. This time the quotas were set at 2 percent of each nationality represented in the 1890 census—a time when there were far fewer central, southern, and eastern European residents in the United States. The law also firmly closed the door on emigrants from Asia, by banning the immigration of aliens ineligible for citizenship. At that point in time citizenship was limited to people of white or Black ancestry. The exclusion of the Japanese resulted in a diplomatic controversy and set back the relationship between Japan and the United States.

The restrictive laws fit with the times. The return to "normalcy" promised by the administration of President Warren G. Harding also witnessed the growth of the Ku Klux Klan. It became a massive organization, both in the South and areas of the North, and its focus was not only on African Americans but also Catholics and Jews. In 1925, an estimated 30,000 members of the Klan clad in full regalia marched in Washington, DC. Anti-Semitism also thrived beyond the Klan, most particularly in the *Dearborn Independent,* a newspaper published by industrialist Henry Ford. Street sales of the paper as well as the KKK paper, *Fiery Cross,* were stopped in Cleveland by order of Mayor William Fitzgerald in the spring of 1921, but his order was shortly ruled unconstitutional.[2] Eventually, and not because of Cleveland, Ford changed the paper's tone.

It was in this background that the concept of the Cultural Gardens came to fruition. After initiating the Shakespeare Garden, which celebrated one individual, Leo Weidenthal, the journalist who had championed the creation of the Shakespeare Garden in 1916, felt there was a need to commemorate wider achievements within cultures. Certainly, the events of the time spurred the creation of the Cultural Gardens. Two partners joined him in the new organization, the Cultural Garden League, which he established in 1926: Charles Wolfram, who was of German heritage, and Jennie Zwick, who, like Weidenthal, was Jewish. Both were active in leading progressive organizations that had ties to the city's immigrant groups. Together they formed the Civic Progress League, which in 1926 became the Cultural Garden League.[3]

Fortunately, Cleveland was still a very progressive city. In 1921, its voters had approved a city manager–form of government with proportional district-based (rather than ward-based) representation.

It went into effect in 1923, and the first city manager, William R. Hopkins, would become a major advocate for the gardens. And the alliances built by the city with ethnic communities during the war provided a who's who roster of potential advocates for the Gardens in various communities. This underpinned Weidenthal's plan to work with groups gathered in various ethnic communities to carry the project forward.

The Cultural Garden League created a representative body, a mini–League of Nations based on ethnic groups. Headed by the leaders of those communities—ministers, judges, business owners, and politicians—the individual groups usually met at churches or an organizational hall. There they selected two representatives to sit on a board that would be responsible for electing officers to oversee the gardens.

Beginning in 1926 with the establishment of the Hebrew Garden, the league and various ethnic communities established a total of 15 gardens (16, including the renaming of the Shakespeare Garden to the British Garden in 1934) before the United States entered World War II. Plans for each would be approved by the League and then by the city, which provided a site in Rockefeller Park. The community was then responsible for funding the construction. Money was raised through bake sales and other community activities, donations from individuals and organizations, and even from foreign governments. Both the Italian and Greek governments provided support for the gardens of their respective groups. With the onset of the Depression, fundraising became difficult, and the city helped support the effort. But the key to the expansion of the system was the Works Projects Administration (WPA), which covered $650,000 of the costs (an estimated half of all expenditures) between 1926 and 1950.[4]

The involvement of public funding opens significant questions as to why public investment was made in the gardens at this time. Was the city's and the federal government's support of the project based solely on a belief in multiculturalism, or was it political? The gardens began to expand at a time when the ethnic vote was becoming increasingly important, particularly when the children of immigrants went to the polls. The 1930s were also the years of the creation of the Roosevelt coalition of workers, immigrants, and African Americans. Because of these issues, it is difficult to determine their motivation

Central to the Hebrew Garden (1926) is this fountain by Georgia Eweh bearing the inscription, "Wisdom hath built herself a house; she hath hewn her out of seven pillars." Dedicated May 5, 1926.

The lower entrance to the British Garden, originally dedicated as the Shakespeare Garden.

The bust of the Bard in the rear of the upper level of the British Garden, created by sculptors Joseph Motto and Stephen Rebeck.

SHALOM ALEICHEM RABINOVICH
CHAIM NACHMAN BIALIK
SHMUEL YOSEF AGNON
SHALOM ALEICHEM RABINOVICH 1859 – 1916
Ukrainian born Yiddish author, playwright, "The Jewish Mark Twain"
CHAIM NACHMAN BIALIK 1873 – 1934
Russian born Hebrew writer, Israel's first National Poet
SHMUEL YOSEF AGNON 1888 – 1970
Polish born Israeli author awarded Nobel Prize for Literature, 1966

with any certainty. However, the fact that 10 of the new gardens came into being after Roosevelt was elected and that 12 came after the city abandoned the city manager–form of government and returned to ward-based representation (with most wards carved out around ethnic or racial enclaves) does hint in this direction.

Whether this question troubled Weidenthal or any of the other founders cannot be answered. But Weidenthal's commitment to the concept of a single world created by the coming together of different cultures is clear. He was moving within and between two concepts of immigration. One was what Israel Zangwill put forth in his play, *The Melting Pot,* which premiered in 1908.[5] It involved the eventual amalgamation of all differences into a single new American identity. Weidenthal was more attuned to the work of Horace Kallen, a Harvard professor and philosopher whose work supported a pluralistic society in which individual cultures would remain intact. In essence, Kallen represented a counterargument to a fully Americanized society.[6] The "one world, many cultures" concept that underpinned the gardens was perhaps best expressed in the One World Festival that the Cultural Gardens Federation would institute in 1945 at the end of World War II. Yet, that one world was comprised of multiple cultures and identities, and the event thus could well be considered a reiteration of the gardens' birth after the First World War.

Facing page: Surrounding the Hebrew Garden court are etched plates bearing the likenesses of significant Jewish poets, authors, composers, philosophers, and religious leaders from around the world.

Certainly, the Cultural Gardens were, in a major way, a reaction to the cataclysm of the Great War, both in terms of a purpose for their establishment and in the way the war redefined national identities in Europe. The Treaty of Versailles re-created the map of Europe through the breakup of Imperial Germany and the Austro-Hungarian Empire. It did the same for the Near East with the carving up of the Ottoman Empire. In an important sense, it and the Fourteen Points put forward by American president Woodrow Wilson liberated ethnic identities that had been subsumed into these empires and provided them with national homelands.

Some of the first gardens reflected this, but they also reflected continuing squabbles among national groups. Seven of the gardens created before 1941 had connections to newly created or re-created countries and their national groups: Slovaks, Czechs, Jugoslavs, Ukrainians, Poles, Lithuanians, and Irish. Yet there were complexities in these new gardens and identities. The Jugoslav Garden was to represent the various nationalities within the newly created

South Slav state. However, the relationships between them were in many ways fractious, and later in the century, the garden, like the nation of Yugoslavia, would fracture. That the Czechs and the Slovaks decided to have separate gardens despite the creation of a nation encompassing both groups reflected the divide that still existed in that new nation and perhaps hinted at the Slovaks' feelings of being forever subordinated—first to the Hungarians and then to the Czechs. Interestingly, the movement to create an independent Czech and Slovak nation was given impetus by an agreement made in Cleveland in 1915 during a meeting of major American Czech and Slovak national organizations.[7] That would lead to another agreement in Pittsburgh in 1918, which called for the creation of an independent Czechoslovak state within which each group would retain a degree of autonomy.

Also reflective of the internal tensions in some of the groups was the process of selecting not only a design for a garden but also those national cultural heroes who would be honored within it. None of the communities in Cleveland were monolithic, and each had divisions along religious or political lines. The Slovenian community, which was to be represented within the Jugoslav Garden (dedicated in 1932), provides an interesting example. It was divided by those who were strongly affiliated with the Catholic Church and those adhering to a left-leaning Progressive movement. The community's two newspapers, the Catholic-leaning *Ameriska Domovina* and the Progressive *Enakopravnost,* were continually critical of one another. Indeed, when the WPA's Federal Writers Project began to select Cleveland foreign-language newspapers for translation and the preparation of indexed abstracts to their content for publication as books, it had to include both papers, despite a standing policy of selecting only one from each community. In one important instance, a bust cast in Yugoslavia and destined for the Garden went missing on its way to Cleveland. Some claimed that it had been stolen.[8]

Dedication of the bust of Ivan Zorman, noted Slovene poet and composer, in the Yugoslav Garden. (Courtesy of the Western Reserve Historical Society)

In some ways, these internal divides were expressed within a larger divide. Arguably the purpose of the Cultural Gardens' network was to validate the important cultural contributions of a particular group and by doing so show its equality in terms of literature, art, music, and governance with the Anglo-American world. The gardens remain, fundamentally, a place where national groups can "show off their stuff." Yet the majority of immigrants who came to Cleveland were not the culturally elite, nor were they—as characterized by historian, Oscar Handlin—an "uprooted" peasantry. Yes, their lives were defined by their language and their own perception of a national identity, but they were also defined by their labor in a system of factories and workshops. Essentially, as argued by Indiana University historian John Bodnar, their lives were unrepresented in the Cultural Gardens with the appearance of one Czech laborer in a frieze in the Czech Garden.[9] The ordinary immigrant would remain unrecognized until the creation, many years later, of the Croatian Garden, which featured a statue of an immigrant mother.

The gardens, while usually associated with a national state, were not limited by such borders. Indeed, the first cultural garden to be established focused on religion and culture. The Hebrew Garden was dedicated in 1926 and would come to focus, in terms of the plaques and monuments erected over the years, on the many contributions made by Jewish individuals to literature, music, and philosophy. But at its core, it was a link to the Zionist movement: the desire for a Jewish homeland. Chaim Nachman Bialik, considered the world's greatest Hebrew poet, spoke at the dedication and planted three Lebanon cedars. Bialik was, at that time, on a tour of the United States in support of the Zionist movement. City manager William Hopkins was also present at the dedication, as was A. H. Friedland, the superintendent of the Cleveland Hebrew Schools. Situated directly across East Boulevard from the Shakespeare (later British) Garden, it mirrored the intentions of its predecessor in many ways. By this time, the surrounding Glenville neighborhood was home to a good portion of the 85,000 Jewish residents of the city. Given this, the garden became a site where noted visitors such as Henrietta Szold, the founder of Hadassah, and Dr. Judah L. Magnes, chancellor of the Hebrew University in Jerusalem, would come to speak at ceremonies.[10]

While the first new garden spoke to national aspirations, the second to be established sought, in a way, to mend a fractured relationship. The German Garden began in 1929 with the rededication of the Goethe-Schiller Monument, which had been moved from Wade Park to the garden site in Rockefeller Park. Its inauguration, slightly over a decade after the United States declared war on Germany, was a watershed of sorts. It reflected the Cultural Garden League's focus on the promotion of peace and, arguably, on the growing doubts of

The German Garden (1927) features a statue of Johann Wolfgang von Goethe and Friedrich Schiller and busts of Friedrich Ludwig Jahn, Johann Sebastian Bach, Alexander von Humboldt, Heinrich Heine, and Ludwig van Beethoven. Dedicated June 2, 1929.

This is the bronze statue of German philosophers and writers Johann Wolfgang von Goethe and Friedrich Schiller.

many in the United States about the nation's entry into the conflict. The city still had a sizable German community, but much of its former internal structure of German-speaking organizations had been fractured by the conflict. There was also a new influx of Germans into the United States, given the substantial quota allotted to the nation and the economic postwar chaos in Germany that compelled many to emigrate. As the garden developed, it would again reflect the strong contributions made by Germans by erecting monuments to Ludwig van Beethoven, Alexander von Humboldt, Johann Sebastian Bach, and Heinrich Heine. The planting of linden trees also carried on the tradition of restructuring the landscape with nonnative plant species particular to a specific nation.[11]

The remaining gardens to be established before America's entry into World War II were all creations of the Depression, and, as noted earlier, many came into being with and because of the fiscal assistance of the city or the federal government.

Many of these achieved a degree of structural monumentality not found in the three earlier installations. The Italian Garden remains particularly noticeable for its position along an access road (Parkgate Avenue) and the manner in which its built structure extends from East Boulevard to what was Liberty Boulevard. The fact that part of its funding came from the Italian government was significant, as it hints at Italy's desire at that time to build a strong international image and to reconnect with its significantly large global community of immigrants. The Italian ambassador was present when it was dedicated in October 1930 as "a symbol of the contribution of Italian culture to American democracy."[12]

With a single exception, the other installations before the war were situated along the east side of the Doan Brook valley with many stretching down the hillside—but none with quite the structure of the Italian Garden. Two, the Slovak and the Jugoslav, were dedicated in 1932, near the height of the Depression. The Slovak Garden represented a large and religiously diverse community, so choosing whom to honor was a complicated process. Two busts, one of Stefan Furdek, a local Catholic priest, and Jan Kollar, a local Lutheran minister, reflect the sometimes-difficult decisions made by the planners from this and, indeed, other communities.

In 1934, two other gardens were dedicated. These represented the Polish and Hungarian communities and were constructed with

The upper entrance to the Italian Garden (1930), with the Renaissance fountain suggestive of the fountain in the Villa Medici in Rome in the background. Dedicated October 12, 1930.

The lower level of the Italian Garden features an amphitheater, winding staircases, and a stone court where summer opera is performed.

The bronze statue of arguably one of the greatest poets of all time, Dante Alighieri, the author of *The Divine Comedy* and the father of the modern Italian language.

The Slovak Garden (1932) is now home to the statue of General Milan R. Stefanik, which stood at Jeptha Drive and East Boulevard from 1922 until 2013. Dedicated October 23, 1932.

Facing page: Ján Kollár was a Slovak writer, archaeologist, scientist, politician, and main ideologist of Pan-Slavism.

1852 REV. JAN 1793
KOLLAR

substantial support from the WPA. The renaming of the Shakespeare Garden might also be considered a new "national" addition to the garden. That same year, as previously mentioned, the Shakespeare Garden became the British Garden, thus moving from a focus on an individual to a broader culture.

The Polish Garden was situated at the corner of East Boulevard and St. Clair and centered around a hexagonal courtyard. That area would be surrounded by busts of noted Poles, including Marie Curie, Frederick Chopin, and Ignaz Paderewski, a globally celebrated musician and prime minister of the independent Polish state. Overall, it reflected the pride in a reborn Polish nation that had been created as a consequence of World War I.

While the Polish Garden reflected a rebirth, the Hungarian Garden—which opened with a magnificent wrought iron gate on East Boulevard that was designed and manufactured by craftspeople who had trained at the city's Rose Iron Works—dealt with a more complex situation. Its first figural image was a bas-relief composer Franz Liszt, and later additions included another composer, Bela Bartok, and writer Imre Madach. Whereas the war had

A view from East Boulevard of the Polish Garden in the 1960s. (Courtesy of the Western Reserve Historical Society)

The Polish Garden (1934) features a sunken hexagonal court encircled by granite walls. At the center of the court is a fountain within a pond. Dedicated October 28, 1934.

PARTICIPATING
CHURCHES/KOSCIOLY
ST. BARBARA CHURCH,
FR. JOSEPH HILINSKI - PASTOR
IMMACULATE HEART OF MARY,
FR. RALPH HUDAK - PASTOR
NATIVITY BVM CHURCH,
FR. ROBERT GLEPKO - PASTOR
THE SHRINE OF ST. STANISLAUS
FR. ERIC ORZECH - PASTOR
AUTHOR
ACTOR
POET
SAINT

Facing page: The bust of Saint (Pope) John Paul II was dedicated on May 18, 2019, with renowned Polish American sculptor Andrzej Pitynsk.

The Yugoslov Garden (1932), now the Slovenian Garden (1991), features a circular fountain and pool surrounded by a paved court. Dedicated December 4, 1932.

IVAN CANKAR

Facing page: The bust of Ivan Cankar, a Slovenian poet and political activist.

The upper level of the Hungarian Garden (1934 or 1938) features a large fountain dedicated to Hungarian composer Franz Liszt and includes busts of Imre Madach and Endre Edy. Dedicated October 21, 1934.

Winding steps lead from the lower to upper level of the Hungarian Garden.

The American Garden (1935) shows signs of the vandalism that took place in the Cultural Gardens in the late 1960s and 1970s. The bust of Abraham Lincoln was placed in storage. Dedicated May 24, 1935.

This bust of Mark Twain, a gift from middle school students at Hawken School, is a replica of the original by Cleveland-born sculptor Frank Jirouch, whose work can be seen throughout the Cultural Gardens.

created an independent Polish state, it had taken away lands from what was the Hungarian area of the dual monarchy, thus leaving a troubled internal situation in that nation, one that spurred revolts after the war and a lingering irredentist movement. Yet the fact that the Hungarian community, like the German community (both enemies in World War I), had become part of the gardens seemed to fit into the goals of its founders: to find unity among difference and value in each culture.

The Czech Garden would follow in 1935, as would the American Colonial Garden (now the American Garden). Occupying a large space along East Boulevard, the Czech Garden would quickly honor Thomas Masaryk, the founder and first president of what was then Czechoslovakia. Later, busts of composer Antonin Dvorak and writer Bozena Nemcova would be added to the site. All of this was backgrounded by a stone frieze that depicted the story of the migration of Czechs to the United States. Within that frieze is an image of a Czech workingman—a rare addition to the Cultural Gardens.

The American Garden over the years would come to host sculptures and monuments to Abraham Lincoln, Mark Twain, John Hay, and Booker T. Washington, along with a plaque bearing the text of the Gettysburg Address.

The appearance of the American Garden, in some ways, indicated a subtle shift away from a focus on immigration. That shift continued the following year with the dedication of the American Legion Peace Garden of the United States.[13] The American Legion, the main organization of war veterans in the United States, created the garden in September 1936 as a reminder of the need for international peace. The legion had come to Cleveland for its annual convention that year, a visit that was boosted by other events in the community, including the Great Lakes Exposition (which included a Streets of the World section that focused on ethnic culture and food) and the Republican National Convention. The fact that Cleveland mayor Harold H. Burton was a wounded veteran of World War I and active in the legion added a degree of gravitas to the dedication.[14]

The dedication came at a time when armed conflict was increasing. Japan had invaded Manchuria in 1931, Italy had invaded Ethiopia in 1935, and civil war had broken out in Spain the year the garden was dedicated. The garden would come to have two

The Czech Garden (1935) features a frieze depicting the history of the migration of Czechs to the United States and a tribute to Tomas G. Masaryk, the founder and first president of what is today the Czech Republic, among others. Dedicated October 6, 1935.

Flanking the frieze are two pylons topped with elaborate sculpting by Frank Jirouch. This one depicts lions, while the other is of eagles.

components, the Peace Garden of the United States and a Peace Garden of the Nations. The Garden of the Nations contained a single monument surmounted by a woman's head representing peace and plantings of trees. Later, during World War II, a bust of George Washington was installed in the Peace Garden of the United States. The primary function of both was to promote national unity and global harmony. The Garden of the United States did so by intermixing soil from each American state on its site in 1939. The symbolism of soil also found its way into the Peace Garden of the Nations. There, in a marble crypt positioned in front of the plinth bearing the female head, nations represented in the gardens placed soil from their homelands into a common vault. That practice has continued to the present, and it is the central ceremony for the opening of a new garden, as soil from the home country is ceremoniously added to and intermixed with that already in the crypt.[15]

One month later in 1936, the Lithuanian community dedicated its garden. It would be highlighted by a three-level design with intricate stonework that gracefully moves from the upper to the lower boulevard. Both the structure and monuments within it reflect on the history of the nation. Once a powerful empire, Lithuania had lost its independence but then regained it after World War I. The lower level of the garden focuses on the time of the nation's rebirth. The first bust dedicated in the garden in 1936 was of Dr. Jonas Basanavicius, a historian and scholar who served as the first president (1918) of the Lithuanian Republic. Cleveland became a center of Lithuanian settlement in the years before the war, and at the time of the garden's creation, many lived along Superior Avenue just to the north of the site where the garden stands.

The last dedication before war again broke out in Europe was that of the Rusin Garden in June 1939. An Eastern Slavic group, the Rusyns (the more proper form of the name) inhabited an area largely in the Carpathian Mountains that stretched between several countries, including the Czech Republic, Slovakia, Poland, Hungary, Ukraine, and Romania. Their community in Cleveland formed largely in the late nineteenth century, and by the 1930s, 30,000 Rusyns were estimated to be living in the city.[16] Beyond their churches and clubs in the city, the garden was the one place where they could not only express their culture but introduce it

The Peace Garden of the Nations (1939) was originally dedicated as the American Legion Peace Garden of the Nations (1936). The garden features a subterranean vault containing the intermingled soil of the nations represented in the Cultural Gardens. Dedicated September 20, 1936.

Sealing the Peace Garden of the Nations vault following the addition of the soil of a new member-nation.

The Lithuanian Garden (1936) pays tribute to Dr. Jonas Basanavicius (the "Patriarch of the Nation") for his role leading to Lithuania's independence in front of the Pillars of Gediminas, the earliest symbol of Lithuania. Dedicated October 11, 1936.

On the upper level of the Lithuanian Garden is the Fountain of Birutė, grand duchess of Lithuania and the mother of Grand Duke Vytautas the Great, one of the most famous rulers of medieval Lithuania.

to the wider community. Its single piece of statuary is a bust of Alexander B. Duchnovich, a priest and poet. The inscription on the bust is simple and straightforward: "I was, am and always will be a Rusin." Although this link to identity was the intent for each of the gardens, it was of particular importance to communities that remained not represented by actual nations and therefore, unfortunately, on the edges of public knowledge.

Three more gardens would be established before the attack on Pearl Harbor. The first, the Irish Garden, was dedicated about seven weeks after the German invasion of Poland. The Irish community of Cleveland was not as large as that of Boston, New York, and Chicago; however, along with the Germans, it was one of the first groups to come to Cleveland and begin to shift the community away from a dominant Anglo-Protestant culture. The Irish Garden, situated immediately north of the Superior Avenue bridge, was constructed as a true garden, one that displayed its identity in its core structure, a series of planting beds within a walkway shaped like a Celtic cross. It was designed by A. Donald Gray, who at the time was considered the city's preeminent landscape architect. It retained that primary design well into the 1960s, when people began adding monuments that honored Irish playwrights and literary figures.

While Ireland would remain neutral during the war, the nations represented in the last two gardens constructed prior to America's entry were severely affected by the conflict. Both the Greek and Ukrainian Gardens were dedicated on the same day in June 1940. They were the last to be built with support from the WPA, which was being closed out as the nation began to redirect funds to focus on rearmament and preparations for a possible entry into the conflict.

Cleveland hosted a rather small Greek community of only 2,350 in 1940. It began to form in the late 1800s, growing in the downtown area and then expanding across the river to what is Tremont today. It would be one of the groups most affected by the quota acts. Its garden, however, really needed no introduction for educated Americans because of the connection of democracy and western civilization to Greece. The garden opened onto East Boulevard with two Doric columns, followed by a sunken planting area that formed the lines of a Greek cross. A Parthenon-style wall that contained the names of major figures from ancient Greece, all well known to the educated public, followed; the plantings, including

The setting of the Rusin Garden (1939) is reminiscent of the Carpathian Mountains of central Europe and is planted with walnut and pine trees. The garden features the bust of Reverend Alexander B. Duchnovich. Dedicated June 25, 1939.

Beneath the bust of Reverend Alexander B. Duchnovich is inscribed his famous quote: “I was, am and always will be a Rusin.”

The central element of the Irish Garden (1939) is the Celtic cross, crafted of paving, grass, and plantings. Dedicated October 29, 1939.

Recent additions to the Irish Garden include tributes to Irish writers and a fountain replicating the St. Patrick's Well in Dublin in honor of manufacturer and philanthropist Fred A. Lennon.

myrtle, also reflected the Greek culture. Four months after the dedication, the Italian army invaded Greece, and in April 1941, the German army invaded as well.

The Greek Garden was the last to be created on the eastern wall of the Doan Brook valley in this era. The Ukrainian Garden would be the first on the west side. Ukraine's history was one largely of rule by or subordination to Russia or the Soviet Union. It had a brief period of modern independence from 1917 to 1919 and then was subsumed into the USSR. Immigration to Cleveland from Ukraine had been largely comprised of workers who settled primarily in the Tremont area. In one sense, the Ukrainians, like the Rusins, were a people without a formal nation, which makes it difficult to accurately estimate the size of the community in Cleveland, given the protocols of the US Census. The garden would break new paths in style. Frank Jirouch, a noted Cleveland sculptor, created bronze plaques and portrait reliefs for the garden. The central statue in the garden honors Larysa Petrivna Kosach-Kvitka, one of Ukraine's best-known poets. The statue remains one of the few in the system that honors women. Three busts in the garden also tested stylistic boundaries; they were the work of Alexander Archipenko. Born in Kyiv, Archipenko came to the United States and was a part of the cubist movement.[17] His busts reflect that in a modest way and, in a sense, presage stylistic changes that would arrive in the Doan Brook valley several decades in the future. Looked at as a whole, the monuments in the Ukrainian Garden reflect strongly on a struggle for national identity and independence. Doing so was a matter of desperate importance for the immigrant Ukrainian population, particularly after a famine engineered by Josef Stalin took an estimated four million lives in Ukraine from 1932 through 1933.

Slightly over one year after the dedication of the Ukrainian Garden, the German army invaded Soviet Russia and in the process overran Ukraine. This created an unimaginable disaster, one that in the postwar era would see Cleveland's Ukrainian population swell as refugees from Ukraine came to the United States.

Five months later, the United States found itself at war following the Japanese attack on Pearl Harbor. During the conflict that followed, the Cultural Gardens and the Doan Brook valley would serve a new purpose—one that enlisted the communities represented by the monuments and plantings along Liberty Boulevard in a search of a common purpose and unity in a nation once again at war.

The Greek Garden (1940) is suggestive of the Parthenon on the Acropolis in Athens. Central elements are Doric columns, a sunken garden forming the lines of the Greek cross, and, in the distance, a pylon resembling the Parthenon walls. Dedicated June 2, 1940.

Winding steps lead toward the upper level of the Greek Garden.

Prominent in the Ukrainian Garden (1940) is the statue of Larysa Petrivna Kosach-Kvitka (poet) and the busts of Ivan Franko (poet and writer), Volodymyr the Great (grand prince of Kiev), and Taras Hryborovych (poet, teacher, and artist). Dedicated June 2, 1940.

The bust of philosopher and statesman Johan Vilhelm Snellman is among those in the Finnish Garden (1958) and was the first addition to the Cultural Gardens in nearly two decades. Dedicated September 14, 1958.

CHAPTER 6

THE POLITICS OF MEMORY

The United States' entry into World War II in December 1941 marked the end of an epoch for the Cultural Gardens. It would take 17 years before another garden was dedicated in 1958, and the existing gardens took on a new role—one that focused more on the need for unity in the United States during the conflict rather than on individual displays of national or ethnic cultures. The German and Italian Gardens now represented the culture of an enemy, while others represented either Allied powers or victims of Nazi Fascist aggression. However, unlike the propaganda of World War I, that of World War II tended to focus on ideologies rather than cultures. It was, at least in Europe, a struggle against Fascist totalitarianism. But in the Pacific theater, the focus was firmly on a people.

The focus on one group of people was apparent in the nation's response to enemy aliens. Only the Japanese, both native and American born, would be confined en masse in internment camps, and the propaganda directed at Japan was based on lurid and negative cultural stereotypes, much like that directed at the Germans a quarter of a century earlier. Absent a large Japanese population (the census recorded only 18 Japanese residents in Cleveland in 1940), the culture was distant from the city's mainstream. But during the latter phase of the war, the Japanese population grew as the government began to resettle nisei from the camps into midwestern cities. Cleveland would become a center for this program, and by war's end an estimated 3,000 to 3,500 lived in the area, with large concentrations in Hough and Glenville.[1]

This small demographic change was eclipsed by others driven by wartime labor needs. With immigration largely shuttered, the nation and northeast Ohio turned to the American commonwealth of Puerto Rico. Many Puerto Ricans came to work at the United States Steel Plant in Lorain, Ohio, and some found their way to Cleveland, eventually establishing a small settlement in the Hough neighborhood. At the same time, Mexicans were invited to come to the United States as temporary workers, or *braceros.* While most would work in the West and Southwest, some labored on railroads in Ohio. Here they joined a small population that came after the 1910–1920 Mexican Revolution and some of whom still worked in area factories.

The major demographic change, however, was the second Great Migration of African Americans. Lured by increasing wartime industrial jobs and driven by the need to escape continued oppression in the South, they, in a sense, resumed the first Great Migration that had been largely ended by the Depression. Cleveland's Black population expanded from 85,504 in 1940 to nearly 148,000 in the Cleveland urban area 10 years later. By 1960, it reached nearly 251,000.

No longer fully confined to the Cedar-Central neighborhood, the Black community began to grow in Glenville, adjacent to the Cultural Gardens in the late 1930s and 1940s. Interracial community groups worked to build trust and improve relations in Glenville in order to keep an integrated population. By the 1950s and 1960s, the Hough neighborhood to the west of the gardens had become predominantly African American.[2]

The war also altered the region's landscape. The construction of industrial plants, in areas once home to vineyards and farms along the railroad lines east of the city, began to drive another wave of suburbanization. In areas such as Euclid, Ohio, villages were now cities. More than anything else, the ubiquity of the automobile as a means of private transportation in the 1920s and the 1930s prompted moves away from the center city, at least until the Depression. But by the late 1930s, movement out of the city it again accelerated. The highway network the city created would have a deep impact on the Doan Brook watershed.

To the south, the city had long focused on plans to extend Chester and Carnegie Avenues from downtown to University Circle. The route on Carnegie was largely in place by the 1930s, whereas the Chester extension took until 1949 to complete. To the north along the lakeshore, the Shoreway—a major limited-access drive that was funded initially by the Works Projects Administration (WPA)—took shape, reaching East Fifty-Fifth Street from downtown in 1938 and Bratenahl in 1941. In 1953, it became an eight-lane, limited-access expressway, bisecting Gordon Park and eventually burying the mouth of Doan Brook into a culvert that emptied into Lake Erie. More important, it turned Liberty Boulevard into a major commuter route, essentially a narrow four-lane thoroughfare, one that served to connect what became known as the Memorial Shoreway after the war with University Circle and from there to eastern suburbs like Cleveland Heights and Shaker Heights.[3]

It was the stark chaos in Europe after the war, however, that ultimately had a large impact on the United States and Cleveland. An estimated seven to 10 million refugees, more than 6 million dead in the Holocaust, a new reordering of borders, and the advent of Soviet domination of Eastern Europe had direct repercussions in the city and within the Cultural Gardens.

The threat posed by the Fascist regimes in Europe had been seen by progressive Clevelanders, many of whom shared the ideals of the gardens, well before the outbreak of hostilities. Knowledge of and work against the Nazi regime and anti-Semitism was not something that came late to Cleveland. In 1933, Rabbi Abba Hillel Silver and Jewish journalist Leon Wiesenfeld began the League for Human Rights of Cleveland after they had attended a national convention of the League for Human Rights and Against Nazism. By the 1930s, Rabbi Silver, who in 1917 came to lead the city's largest—and at one time the nation's largest—Reform congregation, Temple Tifereth Israel. He rapidly became a noted public figure in Cleveland, as well as a leader in the global Zionist movement. Located near the western bank of Doan Brook, his congregation's new synagogue dedicated in 1924 remains a landmark in University Circle.

Buttressed by a letterhead committee of 60 Clevelanders, including many of a progressive stance, and led by a committee of 15 from the Jewish community, the league represented, in substantial part, the ethos behind the Cultural Gardens. It ran a boycott of products produced in Nazi Germany, investigated and exposed right-wing and pro-Nazi organizations, and more generally worked to confront bias and discrimination in the city, partnering with organizations such as the local NAACP. One of its efforts was the publication of a magazine, *This Is Cleveland,* from 1944 to 1946 (when the league ceased operations). The magazine focused on the ethnic groups in the community and, like the gardens, argued for the values of multiculturalism. Its issue on the Black population of the city was a milestone. Outside of coverage in an unpublished Cleveland city guide and an unpublished anthology "The Peoples of Cleveland"—each created by the WPA—little had been written for potential public reading on local Black history. *This Is Cleveland* stood alone as a powerful public argument for equality and comity between the races.[4]

In the immediate postwar period, the city seemed to accommodate a rapidly changing population. It created the Community Relations Board in 1945, passed a law banning discrimination in public places after a protest at Euclid Beach Park in 1947, and passed fair employment practices ordinances in 1950. In sports, the Cleveland Browns football team had two African American players when it began to play in the All-American Football Conference in 1946, and its baseball team was the first American League team to integrate in 1947. A 1954 postwar issue of *Jet,* a popular African American magazine, featured a cover story titled, "Cleveland: The Friendly City to Negroes."[5] Matters seemed to be moving in the right direction.

The postwar period also saw a small, yet significant, influx of new Europeans who arrived because of two federal programs to assist refugees: the Displaced Persons Act of 1948 and the Refugee Relief Act of 1953. Neither replaced the quota system, and the refugee act actually "mortgaged" incoming refugees against their future annual quotas. Those who came to the city included Ukrainians, Germans, Slovenes, Serbs, Croats, and Jews. The laws were responses to huge ongoing refugee issues after the war, but they also reflected the imperatives of a new ideological conflict—the Cold War. That conflict would color the way the Cultural Gardens were seen for the next several decades.

With the World War II over, the gardens returned to celebrating global diversity focusing on diverse cultures and "one world"; a core theme: many peoples, one world. In 1946, the Cultural Gardens Federation began One World Day, a major annual festival that includes parades, foods, and performances that showcase the city's nationalities. The Cultural Gardens also played a large role in the celebration of the city's sesquicentennial the following year—a celebration that included significant participation by ethnic communities and helped to institutionalize the One World Day celebrations.[6]

Yet until 1958, no new gardens had been established; only three—the Finnish (1958), the Estonian (1966), and the Romanian (1967)—were dedicated between 1958 and 1977. Older gardens periodically added new sculptures and plantings, and the Hebrew Garden especially became a site for celebration after the creation of the state of Israel in 1948.[7] Rabbi Abba Hillel Silver would play a significant role in the establishment of the Jewish state.

Despite the lack of substantive growth, the gardens still garnered political attention. Cleveland's mayors came from ethnic backgrounds that reflected the diversity of the city. Frank Lausche, a Slovene, would follow Harold Burton (who later became a Supreme

Celebrating the 28th Annual One World Day program at the Polish Garden. (Courtesy of the Western Reserve Historical Society)

The Chinese Garden (1985) was modeled after the Chinese imperial palace and is guarded by two Chinese dragons. Dedicated April 1, 1985.

Court justice) into office. He would be followed by Thomas Burke, who was of Irish descent. Anthony Celebrezze, Italian born, served five terms as mayor from 1953 to 1962 and then went to Washington to become the secretary of Health, Education, and Welfare. He was replaced by Ralph Locher, who had been born in Romania. Each courted the city's ethnic voters and, like many area politicians, took a patriotic stance during the Cold War. Locher, in particular, championed the creation of the Romanian Garden, which features a statue of Romanian composer George Enescu.

Two other local politicians of Czech heritage, future mayor Ralph J. Perk and Congressman Charles Vanik, played a role in urging President Dwight Eisenhower to create Captive Nations Week in 1959. The event, which is still held, initially focused on the plight of nations behind the Iron Curtain.[8] Various gardens would become the setting for political speeches and commemorations that were focused on the topic. They were appropriate sites, given that many had busts and plaques that honored those who had built what had been an independent cultural and national identity for countries such as Lithuania, Czechoslovakia, and Poland. Essentially, these gardens became potent symbols in another war, and the cultures they represented served as adjuncts to American interests. The creation of the Estonian Garden in 1966 fit directly into this zeitgeist. Its main monument is a figural flame representing hope for freedom. It boldly referenced the fact that Estonia had been forcibly annexed by the Soviet Union in 1940. The Finnish Garden—which has the busts of noted composer Jean Sibelius, poet Elias Lonnrot, Finnish national anthem author Johan Runeberg, and statesman Johan Snellman—might also be seen in this perspective because of its border with the Soviet Union. Similarly, the Romanian Garden might also fit into this time, but its dedication in 1967, at a time of racial strife in the city, and its sponsorship by the mayor suggest that it was a symbolic reinvestment in the gardens at a difficult time. Less subtle and perhaps the most potent reminder of the Cold War in Cleveland was not a monument but a Nike Missile installation just to the north of the Cultural Gardens that had been installed in the mid-1950s along Cleveland's lakefront near the mouth of Doan Brook.

The politicization of the Cultural Gardens during the Cold War in some ways seemed antithetical to their core purpose, one that was

Following pages: This is the lone element in the Romanian Garden (1967): a statue of George Enescu, composer, pianist, violinist, and conductor, who is regarded as among the greatest musicians in Romanian history. Dedicated November 23, 1970.

Central to the Estonian Garden (1966) is this abstract sculpture with an inscribed flame at its center, created by sculptor Clarence E. VanDuzer. The inscription is taken from the epic poem *Kalevipoeg,* written by Friedrich Reinhold Kreutzwald more than a century earlier. Dedicated June 19, 1966.

GEORGE ENESCU
1881 - 1955
WORLD KNOWN ROMANIAN COMPOSER
VIOLIN VIRTUOSO AND CONDUCTOR

"One day the age will dawn
when all torches,
at both their ends burst into flame.
Then the son of Kalev
will come home,
to bring happiness
and build Estonia's life anew."
From the epic poem Kalevipoeg
compiled by FR. R. Kreutzwald

proclaimed in the first full history that covered their establishment and growth. Clara Lederer's *Their Paths Are Peace* was published in 1954, at a time when the creation of the gardens was still in living memory. Although Charles Wolfram had died in 1951, his cofounders of the Cultural Garden League, Leo Weidenthal and Jennie Zwick, were still alive, as were many of those who had served on garden planning committees or representatives to the league or Cultural Gardens Federation. During the 38 years Lederer's book chronicles, the gardens had grown substantially, albeit mostly during the single decade of the 1930s, when there were federal funds available for their construction. They had also come to symbolize the striving for unity within diversity, and they substantially altered a portion of the city's landscape. With two possible exceptions, the American Legion Peace Garden of the United States and a boulder from the Isonzo Front of World War I displayed in the Italian Garden, they did not represent or derive from military heroes or militarism—this despite being situated along a boulevard that memorialized the city's losses in World War I. Yet it remained impossible to limit their political use during a hot or cold war, so potent was their symbolism. But beyond that, there were other more substantive issues confronting the landscape. The demography and spatial geography of the community were shifting, and each posed a challenge to the Doan Brook valley and the monuments and memorials it contained.

In 1950, Cleveland reached its peak population of 914,808. Its industrial economy seemed strong, and it appeared to be working to accommodate racial change. While the percentage of foreign-born Clevelanders, 25.5 percent, was still high, it was the lowest since the 1850s. The lack of immigration, due in large part to the quota law, was a major factor. By 1960, immigrants would constitute only 11 percent of the city's total. While there had been an influx of displaced people and refugees in the late 1940s and early 1950s, it was not large enough to make a difference. However, what really mattered was the movement to the suburbs, where a good number of the refugees and displaced persons eventually ended up along with older immigrants and their descendants. By 1960, the number of people living in Cuyahoga County outside of the city's boundaries totaled 771,815, slightly less than the 876,050 in the city.[9]

Suburban growth was driven by a variety of factors, and possibly the most important were automobile ownership and the creation

The American Legion Peace Garden of the United States (1939) consists of this bust of George Washington and a stone pedestal, which originally included a bronze plaque. Dedicated September 20, 1936.

The replacement plaque in the American Legion Peace Garden of the United States.

of limited-access highways. The highways also carved out sections of older city neighborhoods and in instances divided long-standing ethnic communities such as those in Tremont. Parklands, such as the Doan Brook valley, and monuments, such as the gardens that once had a visceral meaning for those who lived near them, became distant—no longer available for daily use but perhaps for a visit now and then. And as the generation of Ellis Island immigrants aged and died, those who had visited the gardens, had worked on the gardens, or had been part of a community of garden supporters waned each year. The meaning of the gardens for those who took their places in the neighborhoods was often not familiar.

For many, the gardens became a blur as they drove by. Essentially, the Doan Brook valley became the site of another link in getting from here to there in northeast Ohio: it was just another exit off a limited-access highway. Somewhat ironically, it was the upper Doan Brook watershed and the neighborhoods of Cleveland Heights and Shaker Heights that managed to avoid being cut up by a freeway. Albert Porter, the county engineer, oversaw the area's highway expansion in the 1960s. One part of the plan envisioned three highways cutting through Shaker Heights and Cleveland Heights with a major interchange positioned near the Shaker lakes, which Porter referred to as "two-bit duck ponds." A successful builder of freeways in less wealthy neighborhoods, he met his match in the heights when citizens exerted pressure to stop the project, in part by creating a nature center on Doan Brook adjacent to the lower Shaker lakes.[10]

How much of the movement to the suburbs was driven by a desire for a better home or by racial bias is difficult to quantify, but the racial change in Hough and Glenville, the areas adjacent to the valley, was rapid, driven in part by real estate brokers playing on prejudices. African Americans also sought homes in the suburbs; as noted in Todd Michney's book, *Surrogate Suburbs,* some succeeded in overcoming the odds in the 1950s and 1960s, despite barriers. And the green space of the valley was as attractive to newcomers as it was to those who had lived there before. But given the absence of any monument to those who now came to live on the edges of the valley, there was not the same sense of ownership or of belonging for them in the city's monument to diversity. The Cultural Gardens were an overwhelmingly European monument.

There was a growing desire to have a representation of the Black community in the gardens. In 1961, the Cultural Gardens Federation discussed the possibility of creating a "Negro Garden." The idea was dismissed with the feeling that African American culture would fit better into the American Garden rather than an independent garden. The gardens' leadership, comprised of older white individuals (many of whom were linked to Ellis Island immigrants), had difficulty in discerning and or understanding a growing sense of Black identity.[11] Soon after, Black Cleveland city councilman Leo Jackson proposed the creation of a Negro Garden, but his idea died in a Cleveland City Council committee. Jackson again raised the concept in 1968, proposing that a memorial to Dr. Martin Luther King Jr. be erected as the centerpiece of a Negro Garden. That proposal also went nowhere.[12]

Eventually, in 1970, the gardens honored American Blacks with the installation of a bust of Booker T. Washington. Sponsored by the Tuskegee Alumni Association, it was placed in the American Colonial Garden (later renamed the American Garden). But it came about too late and was perhaps not the right choice, nor was it in the right place, given the times.

As the Black population grew in number in Cleveland and particularly in areas along the Doan Brook watershed in the early 1960s, fights among Black and white youth took place in and around Rockefeller Park. In June 1966, white supremacists painted anti-Black graffiti, swastikas, and Ku Klux Klan symbols on buildings and benches in Rockefeller Park. In the wake of that desecration, 22 monuments were then defaced with Black Power slogans.[13] Tensions in the area were exacerbated by long-standing issues in the then largely Black Hough neighborhood, including poor housing conditions in subdivided rental properties, poor city services, and diminishing job opportunities in a city that was beginning a period of deindustrialization and where union membership was often not open to Blacks. These issues came to a head on July 18, 1966. Violence broke out in the neighborhood when a white bar owner refused to provide water to a Black patron and then placed a provocative sign in the window. Crowds gathered, the police arrived, and for three days the neighborhood was a scene of protest, violence, and death. The National Guard was called in. But matters would never return to whatever one might consider normal.[14]

Dedicated in 1970 in the American Garden, the bust of Booker T. Washington represents the first of a Black individual within the Cultural Gardens.

The African American Garden (1977) remained undeveloped until 2016, when planning began for a three-phase project to tell the story of the past, present, and future of the African American community. Dedicated October 23, 1977.

The following year, the city again made national headlines—this time for the election of Carl B. Stokes as the first African American mayor of a major American city. He won by carrying many white votes in a still mostly white electorate. His election fostered hope that the racial divide in the city could be healed. All seemed well until July 23, 1968, when a shoot-out between Black nationalists and the Cleveland police occurred in Glenville. It and the violence that followed left 22 casualties, including seven deaths. Mayor Stokes removed white police from the area, and Black patrolmen and Black community leaders quelled the violence. But the divisions in the city were now more palpable than ever and visible on both sides of the Doan Brook valley.[15] The gardens were literally and figuratively in the center of this division.

The immediate and long-term effect on the lower part of the Doan Brook watershed, on Rockefeller Park, and on the Cultural Gardens was devastating. Visitation dropped because of the violence, and "white flight" from the nearby neighborhoods and the city increased. All of this also reflected the major issues of the time: an increasingly unpopular war in Vietnam, assassinations, environmental degradation, and the ongoing struggle for equality for African Americans and women. How the gardens would or could accommodate these challenges was an open issue, the complexity of which was represented by the bust of Booker T. Washington. He was no longer the man of the hour, and given this, his bust was twice blown up in the early 1970s. Who exactly was to blame remains debatable.

The issues that faced the gardens strongly argued for change. That change would eventually and arguably come about because of actions taken in Washington, DC. Federal legislation passed during the mid-to-late 1960s and early 1970s would not only begin to transform American society by guaranteeing civil rights and voting rights, but it would also set a new path for the future of the Cultural Gardens and natural resources, such as Doan Brook, through laws that finally ended the discrimination entailed in the quota laws and that set new standards for the environment. It would not happen quickly, but when it did, the Cultural Gardens would, in a sense, be reborn.

CHAPTER 7

NO LONGER ELLIS ISLAND

By 1962, the mouth of Doan Brook had gone underground into a culvert that took it beneath the Shoreway (which had become part of the growing interstate system) and into Lake Erie. But more was to happen. The city sank two 500-foot ore freighters just to the west of the brook to form a cheap, effective breakwater to protect boat docks to the west. Eventually an area of the lake east of the freighters would become a dumping ground, initially filled with an estimated 8,000 scrap automobiles and tons of garbage that were taken to the site and burned. Then, with some irony, following the passage of the Clean Water Act in 1972, the toxin-laden muck dredged from the Cuyahoga River was dumped into an 80-acre enclosure at the site. It was a questionable decision, but it was safer than dumping the material into the open lake, which had previously been the case. By 1999, the site was full—5.66 million cubic yards of dredged material had been deposited near what was the site of the mouth of Doan Brook.[1] Today, the site, Dike 14, is a much-visited nature preserve.

In some ways, the story of the transformation at the mouth of Doan Brook echoes the concurrent transformation of the Cultural Gardens. After the racial clashes in Hough and Glenville, the gardens went into a period of deep decline. Busts and other installations were vandalized or stolen and sold for scrap. Perhaps half of the materials in the gardens were lost. To safeguard what remained, many were removed and put into secure storage in the city greenhouse at the north end of the park. The leadership of the Cultural Gardens began to look at simply preserving them as a collective landmark, rather than envisioning possible future growth.[2]

As the city lost industry and population, tax revenues plummeted, and city services diminished. Rockefeller Park became an ill-kept wasteland by the early 1980s, the lagoon at its south end was half empty and choked with weeds.[3] While the One World Day festival persisted, there seemed no easy solution to the crisis. The gardens were usually empty, and many were absent the volunteers who for years had worked to keep them clean. Yet in the early 1960s, a major governmental decision set in motion what would amount to the revival and, in some sense, the reinvention of the gardens.

Emanuel Celler, a New York congressman, was a major catalyst in this change. He was descended from four German immigrant grandparents, three of whom were Jewish and the fourth Catholic. In 1923, Celler won election to the US House of Representatives. Representing New York's Tenth Congressional District, which encompassed parts of Brooklyn and Queens, he was at the Capitol in 1924 when the quota act was passed, a piece of legislation that he strongly opposed and that he voted against. He clearly sensed its discriminatory nature; for the next 40 years, he fought against what he felt was a very problematic law. In 1965, he was still in the House (he would serve nearly 50 years in total). Together with Michigan senator Phillip Hart, he sponsored a new bill, the Hart-Celler Act. Better known as the Immigration and Nationality Act of 1965, it won approval. It set up a nondiscriminatory system of immigration, open to all, with equal quotas for any nation and with an overall annual total for the Eastern Hemisphere and later also for the Western Hemisphere. When initially proposed, the bill focused on employment as the prime factor for allowing an immigrant entry into the United States. Thanks to Ohio congressman William Feighan of Lakewood, the final form of the bill made family reunification the principal factor in determining who could enter the country.

When President Lyndon Johnson signed the bill into law on Liberty Island, the home of the Statue of Liberty, he noted: "This bill that we will sign today is not a revolutionary bill. It does not affect the lives of millions. It will not reshape the structure of our daily lives, or really add importantly to either our wealth or our power."[4] He was mistaken. Like many, he believed the new act would largely lead to the long-delayed reunification of families from Europe and that Europe would continue to be the main source of immigration. The act came into force in 1967, the year that the man who conceived the concept of the gardens, Leo Weidenthal, died. For the first five years, Europe did remain the primary source of immigration, but by the mid-1970s, the entire world was in motion, and the sources shifted to South America, the Middle East, and Asia.

The new immigration law was embedded in a larger context—it joined other Great Society legislation such as the Civil Rights Act of 1964, the Voting Rights Act of 1965, and the creation of Medicare and Medicaid. Together, this legislation promised a new equality for those in America and those who sought to come. These laws, more than any other factor, would reiterate the founding goals of the Cleveland Cultural Gardens as well as ultimately reshape its cultural content to reflect what might be considered an ever-growing, post–Ellis Island immigration legacy. Other legislation passed during this period, such as the creation of the Environmental Protection Agency in 1970 and the Clean Water Act of 1972, would bring new attention to the importance of waterways, such as Doan Brook, and the landscape in which they existed. This growing concern for the environment was, perhaps, best represented by another event, Earth Day, which first took place in 1970. However, change did not come immediately.

When Mayor Carl Stokes declined to run for a third term in 1971, Ralph J. Perk, a Republican politician with strong "ethnic credentials," won the following election. His victory was linked in part to that of Richard Nixon in 1968 and to the concept of the silent majority, which, loosely defined, was the white and ethnic blue-collar voter. There was a reawakening of ethnic identity in the United States, one that was best chronicled in Michael Novak's *The Rise of the Unmeltable Ethnics* (1972). The movement was powerful enough to occasion the passage of the federally funded Ethnic Heritage Studies Program Act of 1972, which fostered the creation of ethnic curricula in the nation's schools. In Cleveland, it encouraged the creation of the Greater Cleveland Ethnographic Museum in 1975. Arguably, this ethnic revival followed the rise of Black identity and Black studies programs in the previous decade.[5]

Whatever its politics, the ethnic revival inspired numerous Americans to search for their roots and ethnic identity—again, perhaps inspired by an African American: Alex Haley's quest for his roots in Africa. This was a factor in the shift away from the melting-pot vision of the nation to one characterized as a quilt or salad bowl or salsa version of a multicultural United States. It was a debatable matter then and remains so now. However, this would benefit the Cultural Gardens later in the century as younger people rediscovered their immigrant roots and began to take up the challenge to maintain and expand the gardens that had been created and nurtured by an earlier generation. This earlier generation included the gardens' three founders Leo Weidenthal, Jennie Zwick, and Charles Wolfram, who had passed or would soon pass away. In many ways, it was a watershed decade.

Nevertheless, the establishment of new gardens was painfully slow. Between 1967 and 2005, only two new gardens were dedicated. The first was the African American Garden, situated on the west side of the Doan Brook valley and dedicated in 1977. It had taken years for this to happen, and when the land for the garden was transferred, it represented an acknowledgment of Black history and culture as a unique and important component within the nation's development.

Booker T. Tall, a professor at Cuyahoga Community College (CCC), drove the effort to create the garden. Tall had created the first Black studies program at an Ohio community college at CCC and was a founder of the Cleveland chapter of the Association for Negro History and Life.[6]

The structure of the garden began to take shape in the early 2000s. Situated on the west bank of the valley just south of the intersection of St. Clair, the garden moves down the slope of the land from Wheelock on the west to the boulevard. Its first segment, the Past Pavilion situated at the top of the slope, focuses the Trans-Atlantic slave trade. As of 2022, the second segment, the Present Pavilion, which extends farther down the slope to the roadway, was planned and ready for construction.[7]

Four years after the dedication of the garden, Liberty Boulevard was renamed as a section of the then new Martin Luther King Jr. Drive, which would stretch from the lakefront nearly to Garfield Park, following a route that had been envisioned decades before as

The first phase of the African American Garden project, the Past Pavilion, is reminiscent of the "Door of No Return," through which we see the Infinity Fountain, suggestive of the tranquility of the Atlantic Ocean.

a grand boulevard linking Gordon, Rockefeller, and Wade Parks to Garfield Park. The renaming of Liberty Boulevard, already a memorial, created controversy during and beyond 1981, the year the legislation was passed.

Unlike the African American Garden, the second addition during this time came with full funding and was supported by a foreign government. The City of Cleveland had an active and growing Sister Cities program, and in 1981 a group from Taipei, Cleveland's sister city in Taiwan, visited. They suggested that the Cultural Gardens include a Chinese Garden; to move the project forward, they raised $500,000 for its construction. Because of the Chinese Exclusion Act of 1882 and the city's location far from the West and East Coasts, Cleveland's Chinese population had never been large. It numbered 155 in 1910 and reached 481 in 1960, nearly two decades after the exclusion act had been revoked during World War II. By 1980, the local Chinese population rose to 1,042 and would grow substantially within northeast Ohio over the next four decades. So, in a way, the new garden was a harbinger of things to come, a time when business and educational connections with both China and nationalist Taiwan would grow substantially. But the proposed Chinese Garden was also a somewhat problematic political statement, because it was a product of a relationship with Taiwan rather than with the People's Republic of China. While the United States did not formally recognize Taiwan as an independent state, it was a growing business partner, and its security was guaranteed by the United States. In a sense, the creation of the Chinese Garden was another reflection of the Cold War.[8]

Facing page: Confucius is central to Chinese culture and to the Chinese Garden.

The offer also raised another matter—the safety of the gardens within Rockefeller Park. Eventually, after a long debate between the city, the Cultural Gardens Federation, and the Chinese Association of Greater Cleveland, it was decided to place the Chinese Garden on Martin Luther King Jr. Drive, across from the Cleveland Museum of Art in Wade Park, and almost a mile away from the main garden site in Rockefeller Park. Its elegant design seemed to fit well into the larger space available there and by its proximity to the art museum; however, its placement reflected on an image of Rockefeller Park as a still troubled, problematic, and dangerous area. During the 1980s, the Cultural Gardens Federation had considered moving the monuments to downtown Cleveland or possibly

installing the sculptures in a secure "Hall of Nations" to be built next to the Rockefeller Park Greenhouse. Neither plan would come to fruition.[9]

Local, national, and international events would continue to play a role in the vision and development of the gardens in the years after 1985. Most important was the shift of the sources of immigration into the United States from Europe to other areas of the world, including the Middle East, Asia, and South America by the mid-1970s. Equally important were the changes in transportation technology. Jet aircraft had supplanted ocean liners; journeys were now faster and soon would be much less expensive.

New and continuing conflicts in Africa, Vietnam, the Middle East, and southeastern Europe, many the outgrowths of the Cold War, created growing numbers of refugees. Despite legal fluctuations as to who or how many might enter the United States, those seeking refuge became an important part of an increasingly diverse population—particularly in Cleveland, with its dwindling number of immigrants choosing to settle in the city.

Whereas Cleveland had been a center for immigration during the period of its industrial growth, it was far less so by the 1980s. Its population continued to decline. It dropped from 573,822 in 1980 to 478,403 in 2000 and 396,815 in 2010, at which time only 4.7 percent of its citizens were of foreign birth. Cuyahoga County's population, which had previously absorbed much of the outflow from Cleveland, fell from 1,720,835 in 1970 to 1,393,848 in 2000.[10] The number of foreign-born citizens in the county had not exceeded 10 percent until 2019.[11] Conversely, the number of immigrants to the United States increased from an average of 424,800 per year in the 1970s to an average of 977,500 in the 1990s.[12] However, those who did come to the city or its county represented a wider variety of national origins than ever before, and some of them would lead a renaissance of the Cultural Gardens and the valley.

Before that could happen, the city had to invest in maintaining its park system. That began under the 1980–1989 mayoralty of George Voinovich, who, like former mayor Ralph Perk, was a Republican with strong connections to the ethnic communities of the city. Of Serbian and Slovenian ancestry, Voinovich inherited a city in deep fiscal trouble: it had defaulted on its loans in 1978 and was losing both residents and jobs. Given his ancestry, Voinovich had a strong interest in the gardens. He eventually was able to secure funds for the upkeep of Rockefeller Park and other parks by initiating a lawsuit against the family of William Holden. Holden had been a substantial landowner in the area and left a will that the mayoral administration argued had not been properly carried out. The action resulted in the creation of the Holden Parks Trust in 1988. By 2010, the trust had provided $4 million toward capital improvements in city parklands, including Rockefeller Park and the Cultural Gardens.[13]

Voinovich's successor, Michael White (1990–2001), also had a strong interest in the park. An African American, he had grown up in Glenville and served as a councilman representing the area. As mayor, he maintained a home on East Boulevard just above the park. With his home under constant police guard, some felt that their presence gave a degree of security to those visiting the gardens. More substantively, during his term in office a four-mile bikeway was created from University Circle to the lakefront along Martin Luther King Jr. Drive in 1997. Named after African American Olympic star Harrison Dillard, the bikeway served to draw a new audience into the valley and, perhaps, did more than anything else to spur new visitation. In many ways, the bikeway echoed the original use of the three parks (i.e., Wade, Rockefeller, and Gordon) at a time when people leisurely strolled the sidewalks or bicycled on the roadway, which was then relatively free of automotive traffic. Only at a slower pace could someone begin to discern details of the monuments and landscaping. Martin Luther King Jr. Drive would later be modified from four lanes to two, which somewhat slowed traffic down and lessened the frequency of accidents, but it still did not cut back the volume of traffic.

Despite these improvements, there still was little activity in creating new gardens until after the turn of the new millennium. When the creation of gardens was revived in the early 2000s, it was the result of many factors, among them the end of the Cold War and the growing presence of new immigrant communities in the region.

The physical catalyst was the creation of the Asian Indian Garden. In hindsight, its roots were deep, perhaps loosely linked to pioneer Asian Indian immigrants such as Shanti Bahdur, an Asian Indian who came to Cleveland in 1927 and established a photo studio in 1933; Ajeet Singh Sood, who was the first turbaned Sikh to graduate from the Case Institute of Technology in 1963; or Paramjit Singh, who came to Cleveland in 1962 and graduated, in a turban rather than a mortarboard, from Western Reserve University in 1965. Each heralded what would be a rising migration from South Asia to the United States, which would truly grow after 1967 when the new immigration law came into full effect.[14]

Facing page: This 17-foot-tall bronze statue of Mahatma Gandhi in the Indian Garden was dedicated on October 1, 2006.

By 1990, there were 5,780 Asian Indian residents in northeast Ohio.[15] Many had come to further their education, while others came to fill necessary slots in medicine or technology. Indeed, the Medicare and Medicaid acts, which passed the same year as the immigration act, built a basis for immigrant practitioners. American medical schools could not graduate enough doctors and nurses to fill the need created by the new legislation, and that brought doctors and nurses from other lands who, once established in the United States with a green card, could use the family unification aspect of the law to bring over parents, children, brothers, and sisters. Many would find work in the city's burgeoning medical system, led by the Cleveland Clinic and University Hospitals.

The actual movement to establish the Indian Garden began in 1979 and grew in momentum during the 1990s. On May 22, 2005, the community dedicated the place for its garden. Located on the west bank of the valley, between the roadway and Doan Brook, it took the spot next to the Finnish Garden where the Chinese Garden might have gone. On October 1 of the following year, the community unveiled a 17-foot-high statue of Mahatma Gandhi. It caught everyone's eye, was easily visible from the road, and, more importantly, was symbolic because of its position near Martin Luther King Jr. Drive. It heralded a new future for the Cultural Gardens, one that signaled a move beyond the memories of Ellis Island and one that began to push aside the racialized fears of the past. The Indian Garden was not only a statement of culture but one of faith.

In the 15 years following the dedication of the Indian Garden, 12 more gardens would come into being, a pace that almost matched that of the years between 1916 and 1940. Five of these represented non-European cultures: Azeri, Ethiopian, Lebanese, Syrian, and Armenian. Another, the Turkish Garden, in a sense bridged Europe and Asia, as does the country. In doing so, it begs the question of the propriety of ascribing a culture to one continent or another.

The Indian Garden (2005) includes six pillars of Indian heritage, the 15 languages of India, and the contributions of Mahatma Gandhi. Dedicated June 22, 2005.

The Ethiopian Garden (2019) features a two-sided mural. As seen here, the front side depicts the history of Ethiopia from the *Cradle of Humankind* to the rise of knowledge and science in *The Modern Period.* Dedicated August 24, 2019.

On the rear of the panel of the two-sided mural in the Ethiopian Garden, *When the Sun Gets the Moon* is a plea from Ethiopia to the world to address overpopulation and fears of the collapse of civilization.

The central element in the Syrian Garden (2011) is the Arabic Fountain with the Arches of Palmyra in the background. Syria's history is depicted on the top surface of the fountain. Dedicated June 29, 2011.

A second view of the Arabic Fountain seen through the Arches of Palmyra from the hillside behind the Syrian Garden.

The Armenian Garden (2010) is shaped like the "vesica piscis," a sacred geometric symbol representing Christ. It is in celebration of Armenia's conversion as the first Christian nation in 301. Dedicated September 19, 2010.

As this plaque indicates, the Armenian alphabet is a result of Armenia's conversion to Christianity.

The planning stage of Turkish Garden. The entrance is marked by two polished rocks inscribed with "Welcome" in English and Turkish. Plans call for a stone image of the Turkish flag and another of two women voting, symbolic of Turkey's democracy and women's rights, respectively. Dedicated October 20, 2016.

Two of the four new European gardens stemmed from the fractioning of Yugoslavia at the end of the Cold War in the early 1990s, as the Serbs and the Croatians decided to leave the Yugoslav Garden and establish their own. The Yugoslav Garden then became the Slovenian Garden. This separation had been, in a sense, prefigured by the internal debates regarding the content of the Yugoslav Garden since its beginning in 1932. The Serbian Garden was established in 2008 and the Croatian in 2012. The latter would eventually install a significant sculpture—a statue of an anonymous immigrant mother and children. The statue in the Croatian Garden perhaps says that each person who chose to immigrate was a cultural hero and deserves to be honored along with the poets, writers, artists, and national leaders represented throughout the Cultural Gardens.

The echoes of the Cold War touched almost every other garden established in the first two decades of the twenty-first century. The Latvian Garden, dedicated in 2006, represented a nation that had recaptured its independence in 1991 from the collapse of the Soviet Union. Dedicated in 2012, the Albanian Garden centers on a statue of Mother Theresa and represents a national culture that had also emerged from behind the Iron Curtain following the collapse of the Soviet Union. It is tempting and perhaps correct to place the fall of the Soviet Union into the same category as World War I and World War II in terms of influencing the nuanced history of the entire chain of gardens.

That collapse had, at last, also made possible the creation of the Russian Garden in 2018—again, one that like the Turkish Garden straddles two continents. It would have been impossible to perceive the creation of a Soviet garden at any time in the twentieth-century history of the Doan Brook valley; yet, it was a hero of the Soviet Union, Yuri Gagarin—the first man to in space—who was given pride of place as the first bust to be installed in the Russian Garden. Almost across the street from the Russian Garden is the Azeri Garden honoring another culture that was once part of the Soviet Union. It was created in large part as the legacy of Heydar Aliyev, the former president of the country who often came for treatment at the Cleveland Clinic.[16]

There is, however, a deeper introspective meaning to the Cultural Gardens, one that relates to the sometimes-troubled relationships

The central plaza of the Serbian Garden (2008) is a reproduction of mosaics found at the Hilandar Monastery (Greece) and at the Patriarchate of Pec and Zica Monasteries (Serbia). Dedicated October 5, 2008.

A second plaza of the Serbian Garden, accessed by a winding path, is dedicated to inventor, engineer, and proclaimed genius Nikola Tesla.

Facing page: The *Immigrant Mother* statue in the Croatian Garden (2012) depicts a woman with an infant in her arms and a young son by her side. It was sculpted by Clevelander Joseph Turkaly and speaks to the experiences of immigrants coming to America. Dedicated June 3, 2012.

IMMIGRANT MOTHER
JOSEPH TURKALY—SCULPTOR

On the second level of the Croatian Garden stands a replica of the Prince Viselay Fountain, representing Croatia's conversion to Christianity.

This fountain, created in the 1920s, originally stood in Willard Park. It was restored and moved to the Albanian Garden, where it was dedicated in November 2013.

MOTHER

Facing page: The Albanian Garden (2012) features this statue of Mother Teresa, sister to the poor, created by Albanian sculptor Kreshnik Xhiku. The garden was dedicated September 22, 2012, in commemoration of the hundredth anniversary of Albanian independence.

The Russian Garden (2018) features Yuri Gagarin, who was the first man in space on April 12, 1961. Dedicated September 8, 2018.

between some of the cultures and nations depicted in the monuments, plantings, and designs that make up each installation. It is something that has become clearly visible as the landscape filled out with the representation of new groups. This increasingly intimate physical juxtaposition often references the manner in which countries that have had long-standing national differences—indeed, animosities—now find themselves side by side along a brook in Cleveland, Ohio. The Armenian Garden is near the Azeri Garden, replicating the geography of the two nations and, perhaps, reminding us of a contentious border. Then the Armenian Garden is situated below the new Turkish Garden, another reference to proximity and tragedy in the Old World. The memories of the catastrophe of 1915 in the Ottoman Empire are still strong, yet those who led the groups that raised funds for and built these two gardens saw no problem in their proximity.[17] Similar is the situation of the Syrian Garden, which was approved in 1929 but did not come into existence until 2011. It is situated directly below the Hebrew Garden. Across the street from the Syrian Garden is the new Lebanese Garden (dedicated in 2019); both reference two nations that were once part of the Ottoman Empire but then and now are divided by religion. The new Pakistani Garden is sited just south of the Indian Garden—again, referencing a division based on religion. But this type of juxtaposition is not new: the Greek Garden stands next to the Italian Garden, and thus here one could reference the conflict between the two nations in World War II.

Then, in 2022, the Russian invasion of Ukraine brought echoes of another international conflict to the gardens. It echoed in both the Ukrainian Garden and the Russian Garden, particularly when the sponsoring group of the Russian Garden decided not to fly the national flag at the site.

More gardens, including Native American, Pakistani, Korean, French, Egyptian, Scottish, Uzbek, Vietnamese, Mexican, and Colombian, have been newly dedicated or are in planning as of early 2022. Their siting will likely expand the system southward, where some of them will join the recently dedicated Ethiopian Garden. Each will add new nuances to the system and, like those noted above, might indirectly reference historical connections, both good and troubling. Dedicated in 2020, the Centennial Peace Plaza, by its name, focuses on a core purpose of the Cultural Gardens. And

This silhouette in the Latvian Garden is of a woman in traditional folk dress and signifies the strength and spirit of the Latvian people.

Central to the Latvian Garden, this arch represents the passage of Latvian immigrants to the United States. It was crafted by Latvian sculptor Ģirts Burvis out of a granite boulder from Latvia. Dedicated October 8, 2006.

The Azerbaijan Garden (2008) features a massive bowl-shaped sculpture made of stainless steel, representing the limits, the containment, the finite, and the boundless openness. Its creator, Khanlar Gasimov, was inspired by twelfth-century Azerbaijani poet Ganjavi and fourteenth-century Azerbaijani philosopher Imadeddin Nasimi. Dedicated June 10, 2008.

it will finally provide a large open gathering spot for concerts and events such as One World Day, which will serve to bring the diversity of the monuments to a common site and focus.

Yet what holds the gardens together, what allows them to be seen as a unit, and what also awakens the visitor to the issues that have divided nations and people is the Doan Brook valley. Certainly, it is now a human-made landscape, and the stream, often bordered by stone walls, is no longer free to carve its own path. But both the stream and the valley make for a narrow, long, linear setting of national cultural juxtapositions that is astounding and deeply provocative. While almost all the small postglacial streams in northeast Ohio have been largely hidden in culverts and forgotten, this piece of the region's natural history has survived and in doing so has become a home to the stories (all much younger than itself) of the multitude of human cultures that have come to make up the city and the nation. Absent the brook and the valley, that story, in all its complexity, could not have been told as well as it has—and as it will continue to be in the future by the Cleveland Cultural Gardens.

Dedicated June 11, 2019, the Centennial Peace Plaza is a 300-seat amphitheater for outdoor events. The floor of the stage features a map of the world and the statement of the Cultural Gardens' mission, "Peace through mutual understanding."

The entrance to the Centennial Peace Plaza has a large pedestal topped with a peace medallion. The medallion features the Cultural Gardens' mission statement: "Peace through mutual understanding."

Founded by the Cultural Gardens Federation in 1946, One World Day draws as many as 30,000 to the Cultural Gardens in August each year to enjoy the food, entertainment, and authentic costumes of Cleveland's diverse cultures.

Chinese student demonstrating his skills
at One World Day celebration

Members of Cleveland's Croatian community in One World Day Parade of Nations

Members of the Latvian community at One World Day celebration

Members of the Great Wall Kung Fu Center representing the Chinese community at One World Day

Representatives of the Association for African American Cultural Gardens representing Cleveland's African American community

NOTES

INTRODUCTION

1. See Sean Martin, "Culture and Politics in Cleveland's Hebrew Cultural Garden," *Middle West Review* 8, no. 2 (Spring 2022): 45–57.

1. THE DOAN BROOK VALLEY BEFORE EUROPEAN SETTLEMENT

1. The best single history of the Doan Brook watershed is Laura Gooch, *The Doan Brook Handbook* (Cleveland: Shaker Nature Center, 2001).

2. David Brose, "Prehistoric Inhabitants," *Encyclopedia of Cleveland History,* https://case.edu/ech/articles/p/prehistoric-inhabitants. Brian Redmond, "The Archeology of American Indians in the Cuyahoga Valley and Northeast Ohio," https://www.nps.gov/media/video/view.htm%3Fid%3D4D888290–1DD8-B71B-0B005BAFDB6B88BE.

3. Brose, "Prehistoric Inhabitants."

4. See National Park Service, "Colonel Charles Whittlesey," https://www.nps.gov/people/colonel-charles-w-whittlesey.htm. This National Park Service site provides a brief biography and cites some of Whittlesey's work on Native American sites in northeast Ohio.

5. Kathryn Flynn, "Vegetation ca. 1800," *Encyclopedia of Cleveland History,* https://case.edu/ech/articles/v/vegetation-ca-1800; Harold E. Wallin, "Flora and Fauna," *Encyclopedia of Cleveland History,* https://case.edu/ech/articles/f/flora-and-fauna.

6. For background on the Connecticut Land Company, see William Barrow, "Connecticut Land Company," *Encyclopedia of Cleveland History,* https://case.edu/ech/articles/c/connecticut-land-co; and Harlan Hatcher, *The Western Reserve: The Story of New Connecticut in Ohio* (Kent, OH: Kent State Univ. Press, 1991).

7. John Milton Holley notebook, Manuscripts Relating to the Early Western Reserve, Mss. 1, Western Reserve Historical Society, Cleveland.

8. William Ganson Rose, *Cleveland: The Making of a City* (Cleveland: World Publishing Company, 1950), 25.

2. THE GOOD EARTH

1. Carol Poh Miller and Robert A. Wheeler's *Cleveland: A Concise History, 1796–1996,* 2nd ed. (Bloomington: Indiana Univ. Press, 1997) provides a good overview of the siting of Cleveland. Original survey maps for the entire Western Reserve are held in the Western Reserve Historical Society's collection of manuscript survey maps.

2. "Doan, Nathanial," *Encyclopedia of Cleveland History,* https://case.edu/ech/articles/d/doan-nathaniel.

3. The place name "Cleaveland" was ambiguous from the time of the initial survey. The spelling "Cleaveland" predominated, but the shorter and now contemporary spelling "Cleveland" was also used. The formal change occurred in 1831 when a newspaper, the *Cleveland Advertiser,* adopted the shorter form. When Cleveland was incorporated as a city in 1836, the legal incorporation document used what is now the contemporary spelling.

4. Ford and White Family Papers Mss. 3666, Container 5, Folder 1, Western Reserve Historical Society, Cleveland.

5. The North Union Shaker community is best popularly documented in, Caroline B. Piercy, *The Valley of God's Pleasure: The Thrilling Saga of the North Union Shakers* (New York: Stratford House, 1951). The archives of the North Union Community are part of the Shaker Manuscripts (Mss. 3944) held by the Western Reserve Historical Society in Cleveland.

3. A PLEASANT RETREAT FROM THE CITY

1. The spelling of the city's name was given both as "Cleaveland" (per Moses Cleaveland's surname) and "Cleveland." It moved to its modern spelling in the 1830s (see "Cleveland Advertiser," *Encyclopedia of Cleveland History,* https://case.edu/ech/articles/c/cleveland-advertiser). Interestingly, the modern

spelling was used in Cleveland's state charter as a village in 1814 and fully legitimized when the community was incorporated as a city in 1836.

2. See Lloyd P. Gartner, *History of the Jews of Cleveland* (Cleveland: Western Reserve Historical Society, 1978) for an overview of early Jewish settlement. For a general overview of early immigration, see John Grabowski, "Immigration and Migration," *Encyclopedia of Cleveland History,* https://case.edu/ech/articles/i/immigration-and-migration.

3. For a good overview of early Black migration to the city, see Russell Davis, *Black Americans in Cleveland: From George Peake to Carl Stokes* (Washington, DC: Associated Publishers, 1972).

4. *The Autobiography of Jeptha Homer Wade, a Modest American: A Transcription and Accompanying Essays* (Cleveland: Western Reserve Historical Society, 2018).

5. Carol Poh Miller, "Parks," *Encyclopedia of Cleveland History,* https://case.edu/ech/articles/p/parks; Carol Poh Miller, *Cleveland Metroparks, Past and Present* (Cleveland: Cleveland Metroparks, 1992).

6. Grace Goulder Izant, *Rockefeller: The Cleveland Years* (Cleveland: Western Reserve Historical Society, 1973).

7. Richard Baznik. *Beyond the Fence: A Social History of Case Western Reserve University* (Cleveland: Case Western Reserve Univ., 2014).

8. "Ernest W. Bowditch," Cultural Landscape Foundation, https://tclf.org/pioneer/ernest-bowditch.

9. Poh Miller, "Parks."

10. Charles F. Schweinfurth is often acknowledged as the city's preeminent architect in the late nineteenth and earlier twentieth century with his work including mansions on Euclid Avenue, churches, and structures on the campus of Western Reserve (now Case Western Reserve University). See "Schweinfurth, Charles, F." *Encyclopedia of Cleveland History,* https://case.edu/ech/articles/s/schweinfurth-charles-f.

4. CREATING A PLACE TO REMEMBER

1. Tom Johnson Papers, Mss. 3651, Container 2, Western Reserve Historical Society, Cleveland.

2. Virginia P. Dawson, "Protection from Undesirable Neighbors: The Use of Deed Restrictions in Shaker Heights, Ohio," *Journal of Planning History* 18, no. 2 (May 2019), https://journals.sagepub.com/doi/10.1177/1538513218791466.

3. "Franco-Prussian War Peace Jubilee," *Encyclopedia of Cleveland History,* https://case.edu/ech/articles/f/franco-prussian-war-peace-jubilee.

4. Lauren Pacini, *Honoring Their Memory: Levi T. Scofield, Cleveland's Monumental Architect and Sculptor* (Cleveland: Artography Press, 2019).

5. Julianna Puskas, "The Magyars of Cleveland, 1880–1930," in *Identity, Conflict, and Cooperation: Central Europeans in Cleveland, 1850–1930,* ed. David Hammack and Diane and John Grabowski (Cleveland: Western Reserve Historical Society, 2002), 159–60; Michael Kopanic, "The Slovaks of Cleveland,1880–1930," in *Identity, Conflict, Cooperation,* 287–88.

6. The story of the debate over the Kosciuszko statue derives from a conversation by the author with Constantine Zielinski in the early 1970s. Kolaszewski did, indeed, foster a split within the local Polish American community that is also chronicled in in Adam Walazek's chapter, "Polish Americans," in *Identity, Conflict, and Cooperation.*

7. See John Higham, *Strangers in the Land: Patterns of American Nativism, 1860–1925* (New Brunswick, NJ: Rutgers Univ. Press, 1962), for a classic overview of movements to restrict categories of immigrants.

8. John A. Garraty, *The Barber and Historian: The Correspondence of George A. Myers and James Ford Rhodes* (Columbus: Ohio Historical Society, 1956). See also "Myers, George A.," *Encyclopedia of Cleveland History,* https://case.edu/ech/articles/m/myers-george.

9. "Weidenthal, Leo," *Encyclopedia of Cleveland History,* https://case.edu/ech/articles/w/weidenthal-leo.

10. Judith Cetina and John Vacha, "World War I," *Encyclopedia of Cleveland History,* https://case.edu/ech/articles/w/world-war-i.

11. Mayor's Advisory War Committee Records, Mss. 3374, Western Reserve Historical Society, Cleveland.

12. Emerson Bodde, "Until Victory Is Achieved: The Cleveland May Day Riots of 1919" (honors thesis, Case Western Reserve University), https://www.academia.edu/32808318/Cleveland_May_Day_Riots_of_1919.

5. EQUALITIES OF CULTURES

1. *Cleveland Plain Dealer,* Nov. 9, 10, 11, 1921.

2. *Cleveland Plain Dealer,* Apr. 17, 1921, Mar. 11, 1923.

3. Mark Tebeau, "Sculpted Landscapes: Art & Place in Cleveland's Cultural Gardens," *Journal of Social History* 44, no. 2 (2010): 329–30.

4. Tebeau, "Sculpted Landscapes," 331

5. Tebeau, "Sculpted Landscapes," 330.

6. John Higham, *Strangers in the Land: Patterns of American Nativism.* See also William Toll "Horace M. Kallen: Pluralism and American Jewish Identity," *American Jewish History* 85, no. 1 (1997): 55–74.

7. Paul Burik, "Cleveland Agreement," *Encyclopedia of Cleveland History,* https://case.edu/ech/articles/c/cleveland-agreement-1915.

8. Tebeau touches upon the matter of the missing Slovenian statue in "Sculpted Landscapes" (334).

9. John Bodnar, "Commemoration in the City: Indianapolis and Cleveland," in *Remaking America Public Memory, Commemoration and Patriotism in the Twentieth Century* (Princeton: Princeton Univ. Press, 1992), 99–100.

10. Sean Martin, *Cleveland's Land of Promise: Rockefeller Park and the Jewish Community* (Cleveland: Case Western Reserve Univ., 2010), 4.

11. The descriptions of the plantings and structure (including sculpture) within particular gardens as noted here and elsewhere in the text is taken from Clara Lederer's *Their Paths Are Peace* (Cleveland: Cleveland Cultural Gardens Federation, 1954) and the Cleveland Cultural Gardens website, https://www.clevelandculturalgardens.org/.

12. "Then and Now," Western Reserve Historical Society, https://www.wrhs.org/blog/then-now-italian-cultural-garden/.

13. The American Legion actually created two gardens. One was the American Legion Peace Garden of the Nations, and the second was the American Legion Peace Garden of the United States. The former would serve as a repository for soil from various nations, while the latter would incorporate soil from 48 states. The American Legion Peace Garden of the Nations was renamed Peace Garden of the Nations in 1939.

14. "Harold H. Burton," *Encyclopedia of Cleveland History,* https://case.edu/ech/articles/b/burton-harold-hitz Accessed October 27, 2021. Dennis Dunfee, "Harold H. Burton, Mayor of Cleveland: The WPA Program, 1935–1937" (PhD diss., Case Western Reserve University, 1975).

15. Part of the ceremony for the dedication of a new garden is the deposit of soil from the homeland into the vault.

16. Michael Metsner, Wendy Marley, and Nicholas Zentos, "Rusyns," *Encyclopedia of Cleveland History,* https://case.edu/ech/articles/r/rusyns.

17. Tebeau, "Sculpted Landscapes," 333.

6. THE POLITICS OF MEMORY

1. Stephen S. Fugita and Henry T. Tanaka, "Japanese," *Encyclopedia of Cleveland History,* https://case.edu/ech/articles/j/Japanese. Thomas H. Linehan, "Japanese American Resettlement in Cleveland during and after World War II," *Journal of Urban History* 20, no. 1 (1993): 54–80.

2. Todd Michney, *Surrogate Suburbs: Black Upward Mobility and Neighborhood Change in Cleveland, 1900–1980* (Chapel Hill: Univ. of North Carolina Press, 2017).

3. Mark H. Rose, "Highways," *Encyclopedia of Cleveland History,* https://case.edu/ech/articles/h/highways.

4. League for Human Rights Records, Mss. 3632, Container 6, Folder 2, Western Reserve Historical Society, Cleveland.

5. "Cleveland: The Friendly City to Negroes," *Jet,* Nov. 25, 1954.

6. Mitch Berbrier, "How Monuments Endure: Public Good Framing as Reiterated Problem Solving in the Statements of Purpose of the Cleveland Cultural Gardens, 1916–2005," *Qualitative Sociology* 36, no. 2 (June 2013): 178–79.

7. Sean Martin, *Cleveland's Land of Promise: Rockefeller Park and the Jewish Community* (Cleveland: Case Western Reserve Univ., 2010), 7.

8. For more information about Captive Nations Week, see Cleveland People, http://www.clevelandpeople.com/events/2020/captive-nations-week.htm.

9. City and county population numbers here and elsewhere come from the *Encyclopedia of Cleveland History,* https://case.edu/ech/timeline.

10. Lauren Pacini and Laura M. Peskin, *Preserving the Shaker Parklands: The Story of the Nature Center at Shaker Lake* (Cleveland: Artography Press, 2016); "The Shaker Lakes Freeway Fight," *Cleveland Historical,* https://clevelandhistorical.org/items/show/55.

11. Berbier, "How Monuments Endure," 180–82.

12. The issue of racial conflict in and around the areas of the Cultural Gardens and as well the inclusion of the Black community in the Gardens is dealt with in some detail in Mark Tebeau, "Sculpted Landscapes: Art and Place in Cleveland's Cultural Gardens, 1916–2006," *Journal of Social History* 44, no. 2 (2010): 339–42, and in Berbrier, "How Monuments Endure," 179–82. Berbrier treats this period in extraordinary detail in an unpublished manuscript, "A Driven Past: The 100 Percent American Story of the Cleveland Cultural Gardens, 1916–2001."

13. Tebeau, "Sculpted Landscapes," 341.

14. "Hough," *Encyclopedia of Cleveland History,* https://case.edu/ech/articles/h/hough.

15. James Robenalt, *Ballots or Bullets: Black Power Politics and Urban Guerilla Warfare in 1968 Cleveland* (Chicago: Lawrence Hill Books, 2018).

7. NO LONGER ELLIS ISLAND

1. "Dike 14," *Cleveland Historical,* https://clevelandhistorical.org/items/show/433.

2. Mitch Berbrier, "How Monuments Endure: Public Good Framing as Reiterated Problem Solving in the Statements of Purpose of the Cleveland Cultural Gardens, 1916–2005," *Qualitative Sociology* 36, no. 2 (June 2013): 182–83.

3. Mark Tebeau, "Sculpted Landscapes: Art and Place in Cleveland's Cultural Gardens, 1916–2006," *Journal of Social History* 44, no. 2 (2010): 342–43.

4. Lyndon Johnson Library, http://www.lbjlibrary.org/lyndon-baines-johnson/timeline/lbj-on-immigration.

5. Timothy Lloyd, "The Greater Cleveland Ethnographic Museum: The Life and Afterlife of a Public Folk-lore Organization," Museum Anthropology Review, http://www.lbjlibrary.org/lyndon-baines-johnson/timeline/lbj-on-immigration.

6. "Tall, Booker T.," *Encyclopedia of Cleveland History,* https://case.edu/ech/articles/t/tall-booker-t.

7. Association of African American Cultural Gardens, http://aaacg.org/.

8. Tebeau, "Sculpted Landscapes," 343–44.

9. Tebeau, "Sculpted Landscapes," 343.

10. Population statistics by year, *Encyclopedia of Cleveland History,* https://case.edu/ech/timeline. "Timeline," *Encyclopedia of Cleveland History,* https://case.edu/ech/timeline.

11. DataUSA Cuyahoga County, https://datausa.io/profile/geo/cuyahoga-county-oh.

12. Immigration statistics are from the Department of Homeland Security Reports, https://www.dhs.gov/immigration-statistics/yearbook.

13. Sean Martin, *Cleveland's Land of Promise: Rockefeller Park and the Jewish Community* (Cleveland: Case Western Reserve Univ., 2010), 10.

14. Poonam Bala, "Asian Indians: Significant Highlights of the Community in Northeast Ohio," *Encyclopedia of Cleveland History,* https://case.edu/ech/articles/a/asian-indians-significant-highlights-community-northeast-ohio.

15. Bala, "Asian Indians."

16. Pietro Shakarian, "Cleveland Cultural Gardens," *Encyclopedia of Cleveland History,* https://case.edu/ech/articles/c/cleveland-cultural-gardens.

17. Author's personal conversation with a founder of the Turkish Garden.

INDEX

Page references in italics refer to illustrations.